CHARTWORK AND MARINE NAVIGATION

For Fishermen and Boat Operators

CHARTWORK

AND

MARINE NAVIGATION

For Fishermen and Boat Operators

SECOND EDITION

GEOFF A. MOTTE

With Thomas M. Stout

CORNELL MARITIME PRESS
Centreville, Maryland

Library of Congress Cataloging in Publication Data

Motte, Geoff A., 1936-
   Chartwork and marine navigation for fishermen
and boat operators.

      1. Nautical charts. 2. Navigation.   I. Stout,
Thomas M., 1935-   II. Title.
VK587.M63 1984   623.89′2   83-46037
ISBN 0-87033-314-3

Manufactured in the United States of America

First edition, 1977. Second edition, 1984

CONTENTS

Exercises—Part I

PART II: MARINE NAVIGATION

Section 1. Principles of Navigation

Exercises—Part II

Appendix: Table Extracts   169

PREFACE TO THE SECOND EDITION

Most of this work remains deservedly unchanged from the First Edition. A few notations in the text have been changed to reflect standard American abbreviation and practice. Many of the exercises have been adjusted to reflect changes in coastal charts since the publication of the First Edition. A small section on plotting sheet construction has been inserted between the Chartwork and Marine Navigation portions. The Loran C system, explained precisely, together with the hyperbolic grid concept, has been added. Finally, the solution of the navigational triangle is done using H.O. Pub. No. 229 rather than H.O. Pub. No. 214. (The navigator who has access to H.O. Pub. No. 214 can still derive perfectly satisfactory and correct solutions to sight reduction problems.)

PREFACE TO THE FIRST EDITION

This book combines two smaller instructional manuals, *Chartwork for Fishermen and Boat Operators* and *Navigation for Fishermen and Boat Operators,* which were initially published by the Sea Grant Program at the University of Rhode Island. The smaller books provided the material for two courses in Coastwise and Deep-sea Navigation, respectively. Every effort has been made to render the text as potentially useful and concise as possible by highlighting the various wrinkles and basics of navigation considered most practical for any ship or boat operator.

The exercises have been tested over a period of fifteen years by student commercial vessel operators and yachtsmen alike. All questions should be attempted as they are ordered by level of difficulty.

Any prudent seaman should be conversant with the elements and practice of navigation in depth, and the writer has attempted to provide a simple route to that end by means of this book.

Part I

CHARTWORK

In order to complete the exercises in Part I, you must have National Ocean Survey Charts 1, 13009 (71), 13218 (1210), and 13205 (1211), as well as a set of nautical tables such as *The American Practical Navigator* (Pub. No. 9), Vol. II, a pair of parallel rulers and dividers, or navigator's triangles. These materials may be ordered from most marina houses or nautical suppliers.

1

INTRODUCTION TO CHARTWORK

In general terms, chartwork is used to plot a ship's progress in sight of land while navigation is a similar process used for ships out of sight of land. Chartwork applies basic geometric theories to a ship's course, speed, bearings, and position lines. Navigation applies trigonometry to observations of celestial bodies and also obtains position lines from electronic aids to determine a vessel's position.

Care of Charts

The mariner uses his chart somewhat as a motorist uses a road map. The main difference is that at sea the navigator plots his own roads, or "courses to steer," on the chart. A chart often costs as little as a dollar, but circumstances often render a single chart the most important piece of equipment on board ship. A chart should never be abused nor used for any other purpose than that intended; the safety of your vessel and all aboard her may depend on a *single* chart.

The following rules should be adhered to:

1. Pencil courses and bearings on the chart lightly but firmly with a soft (No. 2) pencil.

2. Keep chart weighted down against gusts of wind which sometimes unexpectedly occur when a vessel alters course.

3. Keep charts flat in a drawer rather than rolled up.

4. Keep charts dry and do not place coffee cups or ashtrays on them.

5. Make sure that your charts are kept up to date by adding corrections published, in the United States, weekly in *Local Notices to Mariners* which are available from each Coast Guard District Office as well as in worldwide *Notices to Mariners* published weekly by the Defense Mapping Agency Hydrographic Center. (*Summaries of Corrections* are also available from this agency and are distributed on request.)

The charts available for a required route can be selected from a chart catalog. (See illustrations on the following pages.)

SAILING AND GENERAL CHARTS

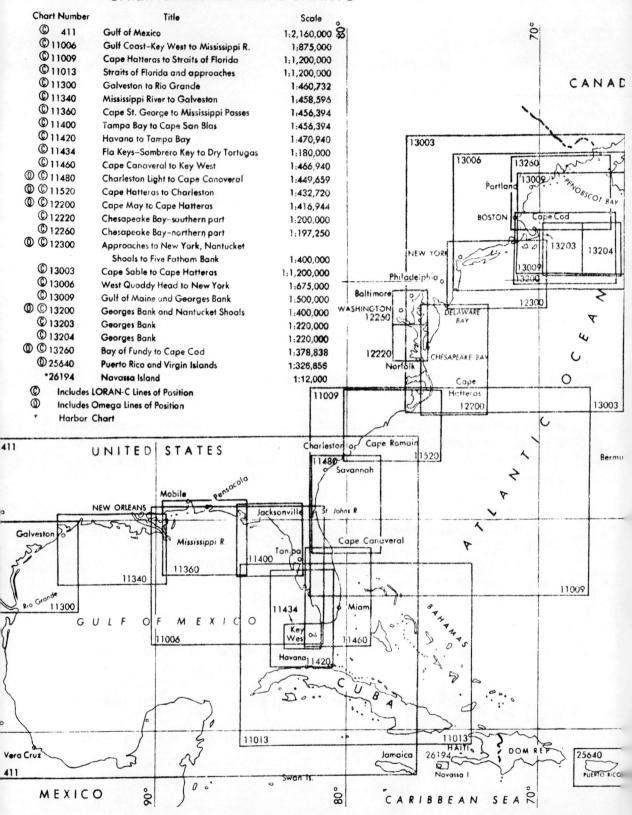

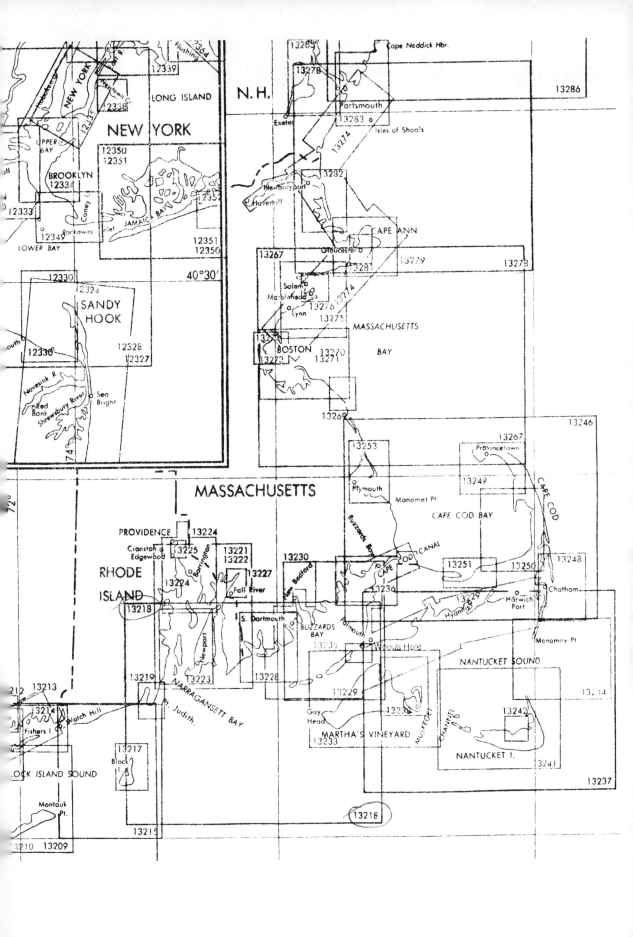

S.20   K I N G F I S H E R   S E I N E   N E T   C H A R T

MORAY FIRTH GROUND

WEST BANK

Clean Area, do not go N. of Sector

Very clean between Fasts do not go N. of Sector

SOUNDINGS in FATHOMS

Edition. Mar. 1966
Corrected to 24 AUG 1967

Compiled under the direction of Skipper F. S. Johnson, for the
White Fish Authority. KINGFISHER CHARTS are published to
record only dangers, obstructions and areas of foul ground which
cause loss and damage to gear and loss of fishing time.
They are not intended for purposes of general navigation.
Where no depths or ground details are shown, there are no known
dangers or obstructions on record.

Published in conjunction with the White Fish Authority by Imray

Compiled from information provi
and based on British Admiralty Ch
Controller of H.M. Stationery Office

Decca Readings of Reported Obstructions Numbered on West side of Chart			
No.	Green D	Purple X	
1	33.60	81.00	Obs.
2	33.60	78.75	"
3	34.00	73.00	"
4	34.70	64.00	"
5	34.78	89.35	"
6	34.80	85.00	"
7	35.05	82.22	"
8	35.05	65.00	S.V.
9	35.25	65.15	Obs.
10	35.50	70.50	"
11	36.00	80.00	S.V.
12	36.20	70.30	Obs.
13	36.60	63.10	"
14	38.40	67.00	S.V.
15	36.61	67.50	Obs.
16	36.70	73.20	"
17	36.90	53.90	"
18	36.86	86.85	"
19	37.31	48.54	"
20	37.80	58.00	"
21	37.80	56.00	"
22	38.85	58.00	"
23	39.30	56.70	Obs.
24	38.30	73.30	"
25	39.80	52.40	"
26	39.80	60.00	"
27	39.90	66.00	"
28	40.05	59.58	"
29	40.10	61.00	"
30	40.05	66.20	"
31	40.15	84.40	S.V.
32	40.15	74.50	Obs.
33	40.30	70.90	"
34	40.30	66.20	"
35	40.90	77.90	S.V.
36	41.00	78.00	Obs.
37	41.05	79.90	"
38	41.25	63.00	"
39	42.00	57.00	"
40	42.20	59.20	"
41	42.38	52.70	"
42	42.40	61.00	"
43	42.40	70.35	"
44	42.45	65.00	"
45	42.95	75.00	"
46	42.95	79.50	"
47	43.40	71.00	S.V.
48	44.00	77.45	Obs.
49	44.55	70.20	"
50	45.05	69.30	S.V.
51	45.10	78.50	Obs.
52	46.90	83.50	S.V.
53	47.00	71.40	Obs.
54	47.04	71.45	"
55	47.35	70.50	"
	D	B	
56	31.35	76.25	Obs.
57	31.45	77.00	"
58	31.90	87.20	"
59	31.90	76.80	"
60	32.00	90.50	"
61	32.00	84.00	S.V.
62	32.00	70.00	Obs.
63	32.90	53.00	"
64	32.60	68.00	"
65	32.80	89.30	"
66	32.70	61.40	S.V.
67	32.90	63.40	Obs.
68	32.90	58.30	"
69	33.10	52.90	"
70	33.40	57.18	"
71	33.45	68.00	"
72	33.50	69.00	"
73	33.58	56.30	"
74	33.80	96.85	"
75	33.90	57.10	"
76	33.90	74.80	"
77	34.40	53.00	"
78	34.48	63.50	"
79	34.50	65.80	"
80	34.50	87.30	"
81	34.75	78.10	S.V.
82	34.80	57.45	Obs.
83	34.80	53.60	"
84	34.80	63.10	"
85	34.90	39.00	"
86	35.00	56.90	"
87	35.05	65.60	S.V.
88	35.15	64.80	Obs.
89	35.25	68.15	"
90	35.35	50.10	"
91	36.00	55.50	B.P.
92	36.00	70.00	Obs.
93	36.20	69.80	"
94	36.40	52.00	S.V.
95	36.90	67.60	Obs.
96	36.95	69.30	S.V.
97	37.10	56.23	"
98	37.50	53.90	Obs.
99	37.68	57.55	"
100	38.05	54.25	"
101	38.15	59.58	"
102	38.65	58.00	S.V.
103	39.00	77.00	Obs.
104	39.50	72.40	S.V.
105	39.65	72.00	Obs.
106	40.00	78.00	"
107	40.15	54.40	"
108	40.25	73.28	"
109	41.10	75.25	"
110	41.20	58.50	"
111	41.70	81.00	S.V.
112	41.70	56.00	Obs.
113	41.80	56.22	"
114	41.90	69.30	"
115	41.90	76.00	"
116	41.90	57.30	"
117	42.62	76.70	"
118	42.52	61.91	"
119	42.50	58.00	"
120	42.70	68.40	"
121	42.70	75.10	"
122	43.02	74.40	S.V.
123	43.05	65.70	Obs.
124	43.12	60.95	"
125	43.20	66.10	"
126	43.20	69.10	"
127	43.20	55.00	"
128	43.40	71.00	"
129	43.50	59.00	S.V.
130	43.90	74.35	Obs.
131	44.00	57.48	S.V.
132	44.50	52.50	Obs.
133	45.40	52.00	"
134	43.90	76.90	"
135	46.15	52.00	"
136	46.86	50.30	"
137	50.80	53.50	Obs.
138	31.80	57.00	"
139	32.40	56.70	"
140	37.43	55.25	S.V.
141	38.08	84.20	Obs.
142	38.30	62.10	"
143	39.00	55.90	"
144	39.28	54.60	"
145	39.28	56.00	"
146	39.55	61.70	"
147	39.80	58.50	"
148	39.98	56.00	"
149	40.03	51.28	"
150	40.10	62.00	"
151	40.70	55.00	"
152	40.80	54.50	"
153	40.98	57.42	"
154	42.00	53.79	"
155	42.00	80.40	"
156	43.18	83.65	"

Chart Types

Charts are commonly termed large-scale or small-scale. When a certain distance on earth is represented by a relatively large distance on the chart, the chart is termed a large-scale chart. A chart requiring less detail, such as an ocean chart, would have the same distance represented by a comparatively small distance and, thus, be termed a small-scale chart.

Chart scale is represented by a ratio, such as 1:200,000, meaning 1 inch on the chart represents 200,000 inches, or about 2.74 nautical miles, on the surface of the earth. (Note that a nautical mile is taken as 6,076 feet.)

$$\text{Note: Scale no.} = \frac{\text{distance on earth in nautical miles} \times 6,076 \times 12}{\text{representative distance on chart in inches}}$$

World Charts

These charts are on a very small scale and used for plotting only main ocean routes. They are not generally used for navigation.

Ocean Charts

These are on a small scale, e.g., 1:3,000,000, and are used for deep sea navigation only. Ocean charts show a minimum of detail.

Coastal Charts

These are used for chartwork and are of a conveniently large scale, e.g., 1:200,000. A good coastal chart shows depth of water and the nature of the ocean floor, both in great detail. All lights and buoys, characteristic tidal streams, and dangers to navigation also are clearly indicated.

Plan Charts

When minute detail is required and vessels may be maneuvering within only a few feet of shoals and rocks, a considerably larger scale must be used, e.g., 1:20,000. Such a scale is necessary for harbors, anchorages, and their approaches.

Miscellaneous Charts

Charts marked with Loran, Omega, or Decca position lines, meteorological charts, and charts marked with lines of magnetic variation come under this category.

Some of the main fishing grounds of the world, such as the Dogger Bank, are specially charted on fishing charts which give such details as "hangups" and seasonal movement of various fish species. The "Kingfisher Charts," produced by the British White Fish Authority, are excellent fishing charts. However, this type of chart should *not* be used for coastal chartwork.

Exercise:
Chart Scales

Answers to all exercises in Part I are on pages 97 to 103.

1. What distance at sea does a length of 3 inches on a chart of scale 1:200,000 represent?

2. How many inches would be measured on a chart of scale 1:470,940 between two points 10 miles apart?

3. If 2 inches on the chart represent 7.3 miles on the earth, find the scale of that chart.

4. What distance at sea do 6 inches on a chart of scale 1:470,600 represent?

5. What distance on a chart of scale 1:80,000 would be covered by a vessel steaming 17 miles?

6. What scale of chart shows a distance of 12½ nautical miles as 3½ inches?

7. If 7¾ inches on the chart represent 54 miles steamed at sea, what would be the scale of this chart?

8. What scale of chart shows a distance of 23 miles as 4.6 inches?

9. What distance would be steamed at sea between two positions 6 inches apart on a chart of scale 1:47,000?

10. If a vessel steams 840 miles, what distance would this be indicated by on a chart of scale 1:2,160,000?

2

BASIC DEFINITIONS FOR POSITION

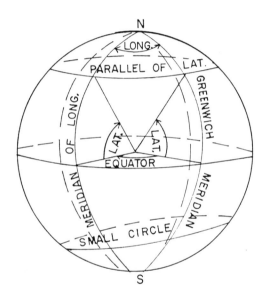

For navigational purposes the earth is assumed to be a sphere. In fact the earth is an oblate spheroid, about 27 miles less in diameter between the poles than at the equator.

Great and Small Circles

A great circle is a circle on the surface of the earth the plane of which passes through the earth's center. If a sphere were cut along a great circle, it would be divided into two equal halves. Should the plane of a circle not pass through the center of the sphere, a small circle would have been drawn.

All meridians of longitude are great circles which pass through the poles. The prime meridian passes through the Greenwich Observatory in England, and longitude is measured east or west of this prime meridian.

All parallels of latitude are small circles drawn parallel to the equator. The equator is a great circle midway between the poles.

Position Notation

Latitude (Lat., L)

The latitude of an object on the earth's surface is the angle at the center of the earth between the equator and the object, measured from 0° to 90° north or south of the equator along the meridian passing through the object.

Longitude (Long., λ)

The longitude of an object on the earth's surface is the angle at the pole between the prime meridian and the meridian passing through the object, measured from 0° to 180° east or west of the prime meridian.

Position

An object is positioned on earth by its latitude and longitude in that order or by true bearing and distance from some reference point nearby; e.g., the whistle buoy in latitude 41-19.3N, longitude 071-28.5W is also 173½° T × 2.4 miles from Point Judith. (See Chart 13218.)

Difference of Latitude (D. Lat. or l)

D. Lat is the angle at the center of the earth between the parallels of latitude passing through the two points considered.

Difference of Longitude (D. Long. or DLo)

D. Long. is the angle at the pole between the meridians passing through the two points considered.

Note that distance is always measured on the latitude scale of the chart. One minute of difference of latitude equals one nautical mile. This will be discussed later.

Exercise:

Position (Charts 13205 and 13218)

1. Find the true bearing and distance of a vessel in 41-21N, 070-53W from Gay Head Lt.

2. In what position would a vessel 6.9 miles due south of Beavertail Lt. be?

3. How would you refer a vessel in 41-22.9N, 071-05W to Buzzards Tower?

4. In what position would a vessel having Block I. Souteast Pt. Lt. bearing 231° T × 7.6 miles be?

5. How would a vessel in 41-22.8N, 071-26.4W be positioned from Castle Head Lt.?

6. In what position would a vessel 161°T × 5 miles from Montauk Pt. Lt. be?

7. Position a vessel in 41-14.2N, 072-10.8W with reference to Little Gull I. Lt.

8. In what position would a vessel 8.2 miles due west of Block I. Sandy Pt. Lt. be?

9. How would a vessel in 41-09.9N, 071-58.2W be positioned relative to Race Pt. Lt?

10. In what position would a vessel 096°T × 16.6 miles from Montauk Pt. Lt. lie?

Make sure that the following aids to navigation are charted as for 1982. Discrepancies in answers to this and all other exercises may result if the charted positions are not as follows.

Light List No.	Description	Latitude (N)	Longitude (W)
42.50	Boston Approach Lighted Buoy BF	42-21.2	070-41.5
52.50	Boston Approach Lighted Whistle Buoy BD	42-08.3	069-53.6
56	Nauset Lighted Whistle Buoy 4	41-56.0	069-53.8
58	Chatham Lighted Whistle Buoy 6	41-41.7	069-50.0
62	Pollock Rip Entrance Lighted Horn Buoy PR	41-36.1	069-51.1
64	Great Round Shoal Channel Entrance Lighted Whistle Buoy GRS	41-26.1	069-43.4
67.50	Boston Approach Lighted Buoy BB	41-15.5	069-17.7
71	Great Rip Lighted Buoy 4	41-07.6	069-42.5
71.50	Boston Approach Lighted Whistle Buoy BA	40-49.1	069-00.0
72	Davis South Shoal Lighted Whistle Buoy 8DS	40-43.2	070-00.5
73	Nantucket Shoals Lightship	40-30.0	069-28.0
76	Squibnocket Lighted Bell Buoy 1	41-15.7	070-46.3
77	Nomans Land Lighted Whistle Buoy 2	41-12.2	070-50.0
83	Southwest Ledge Lighted Bell Buoy 2	41-06.7	071-40.3
609	Vineyard Sound Junction Lighted Whistle Buoy VS	41-22.6	071-00.2
678.51	New Bedford Harbor Approach Lighted Buoy 1	41-31.8	070-50.9
799	Point Judith Lighted Whistle Buoy 2	41-19.2	071-28.5
902	Cerberus Shoal Lighted Whistle Buoy 9	41-10.4	071-57.2
906	Endeavor Shoals Lighted Gong Buoy 3	41-06.0	071-46.3
907	Shagwong Reef Lighted Bell Buoy 7SR	41-06.9	071-54.9
1319	Gardiners Island Lighted Bell Buoy 1GI	41-09.0	072-09.0
Canadian	Brazil Rock Lighted Whistle Buoy	43-21.0	065-26.5
Canadian	Gannet Rock Lighted Bell Buoy 70Y	43-36.6	066-12.4
Canadian	Gull Rock Lighted Whistle Buoy	43-36.6	065-02.5
Canadian	Lurcher Shoal Lighted Whistle Buoy LURCHER	43-47.5	066-37.5

If any one of these aids to navigation is not charted in the position given above, correct your chart accordingly and enter this notation in the lower left-hand corner of your chart:

This chart is not to be used for navigational purposes. It has been corrected for book exercises only.

3

FIXING POSITION NEAR LAND

The position of a vessel should be constantly fixed, or determined, by as many different means as possible. This is best done by checking positions obtained from crossed bearings of shore objects with information from radar, the radio direction finder, the echo sounder, and other navigational instruments.

Bearings are obtained by looking across the top of the compass card at a shore object through a sighting vane or through a reflecting prism mounted on a rotatable frame over the compass; this device is called an azimuth mirror.

Sometimes hand-bearing compasses or pelorus cards are used to take bearings. A hand compass has a handle underneath it and a prism on top. The bearing of a shore object is noted, and the difference in direction of the hand compass and ship's compass is noted and applied. A pelorus is simply a small compass card which is set up in the fore and aft line to coincide with the ship's compass. A bearing can be taken by means of a set of two vanes which move on a diameter across the card.

A single bearing gives only a position line, somewhere along which the vessel must be situated. A fix is obtained when additional information determines just where on the position line the vessel lies. Another bearing, a radar distance from the land, or a sounding would give this information and complete the fix.

When two bearings are crossed for a fix, their angle of intersection should be as near to 90° as possible. When the angle is very small, a slight error in the bearing may give a large error in position. For accuracy a fix should be checked with a third position line bearing. Often the three bearings will not meet at a single point but will form a small triangle known as a "cocked hat." In this case it is advisable to position the vessel in the corner of the cocked hat nearest to danger.

The Loran C Hyperbolic Navigation System

Significant changes have taken place involving electronic aids to navigation since the time this book was first published. Loran A, which was used extensively by fishermen and boat operators on both coasts of the United States, has been phased out to be replaced by the more versatile Loran C hyperbolic navigation system. There are a vast number of boats utilizing Loran C. Therefore it is desirable to contain a brief

Chartwork Instruments

Dividers

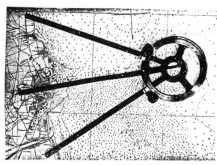

Parallel Rules

Station Pointer

Log Clock

Marine Sextant

Compass

Azimuth Mirror

Hand-bearing
Compass and Prism

Pelorus Card

Liquid Compass
with Combined Azimuth
and Steering Prism

description of the system in this book, as well as incorporating practical examples of its use in some of the chartwork exercises.

Hyperbolic navigation systems such as Loran, Decca, or Omega are based on the measurement of the difference in time and/or phase of radio wave reception from signals received from a master transmitting station and a slave station. A constant signal difference will form a hyperbolic line as shown in simplified form in the following diagram and evidenced on the Loran C charts to be used for the various exercises herein contained.

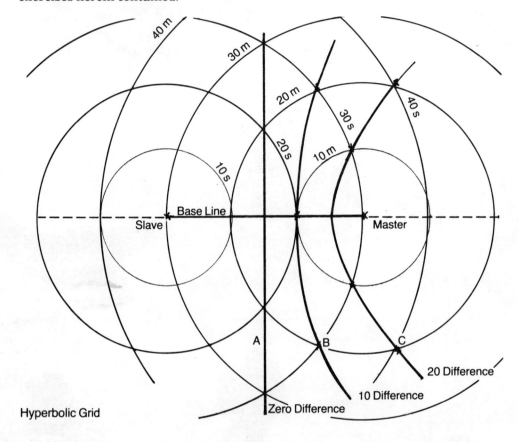

Hyperbolic Grid

Lines A, B, and C are typical position lines generated by a Loran system to form the Loran grid which is superimposed on the appropriate navigational chart. Line A which has a zero difference in effective time difference between the receipt of master and slave signals is known as the base line perpendicular. Dotted lines indicate the base line extension which is the most unreliable part of the grid, since signal differences either side of the line are similar, leading to possible ambiguity. Lines B and C are the hyperbolic lines of 10 and 20 difference respectively between the two transmitted signals.

Loran C is a multipulse long-range navigational aid which operates on a central carrier frequency of 100 kilocycles, i.e., wavelength of 3,000 meters (note that the product of wavelength in meters and the frequency in thousands of cycles per second is a constant 300,000). Loran C transmission consists of a multipulse burst of 9 pulses from the master station and 8 pulses from the slave station in a wave train with individual pulses spaced 1,000 microseconds apart. Multipulse is used to give more signal energy at the receiver thereby increasing signal-to-noise ratio. The pulse itself is about 300 microseconds in duration and at the 90-110 kilocycle range of frequency has the particular characteristics that allow not only simple comparison of the time difference between receipt of the master pulse train and the slave pulse train but also manipulation and examination of the pulse envelope (known as cycle matching) to give a high degree of system accuracy and dependability. In general these basic characteristics result in a system range of up to 1,200 miles on ground-wave transmission with an average accuracy of about one-eighth to one-fourth of a mile.

A Loran C network may have 1 master station and up to 3 slave stations which are triggered by the master signal in order that a receiver anywhere within the gridzone must first receive the master signal and sometime later a selected slave signal. The system is also characteristically suited to the Phase-Coding Identification process which assigns a positive or negative bias to each pulse within a station's transmitted wave train which allows the Loran receiver on shipboard to lock automatically into and distinguish the incoming wave trains, one from another.

Thus the navigator has simply to dial the specific grid required by consulting the chart and then plot the result. However, at all times it must be remembered that Loran C is just another *aid* to navigation. It is prone to error and breakdown. The fundamental processes of navigation and chartwork are irreplaceable and allow for checking and double-checking information received from aids to navigation as well as ensuring that information from such aids are used to the fullest extent and in the most effective manner.

Exercise:
Fixing Position (Chart 13205) ans p. 97

1. Find the position and depth of water of a vessel having Montauk Pt. Lt. bearing 302° T and Southeast Pt. Lt. bearing 044° T.

2. Find the position and depth of water when Watch Hill Pt. Lt. bears 306° T and Sandy Pt. Lt. bears 073° T.

3. Give position of a vessel having East Hampton Spire and Flagstaff in range and the nearby Aeronautical Lt. bearing due north.

4. Find position of a vessel with Montauk Pt. Lt. bearing 331° T in 30 fathoms of water.

5. Find the position of a vessel with Montauk Pt. Lt. in range with Star I. Tower Lt. and Little Gull I. Lt. bearing 339½° T. What sounding would you expect in this position?

6. Give the position of a vessel having Watch Hill Pt. Lt. bearing 295° T, Point Judith Lt. bearing 055° T, and Montauk Pt. Lt. bearing 215° T.

7. What sounding would you expect in a position with Point Judith Lt. bearing 065° T on Loran position line 9960-W-14580? What distance from the nearest land should the radar indicate?

8. Give position of a vessel with Montauk Pt. Lt. bearing 318° T if the radar gives the distance from nearest land as 9 miles.

9. A vessel steering due north, true course, observes Montauk Pt. Lt. 30° on the starboard bow while crossing the 20-fathom line. Find her position.

10. Where would you position a vessel on a course of 225° T having Race Pt. Lt. bearing 035° T, Great Gull I. Tower bearing 007° T, and Plum I. Tank bearing 306° T?

4

READING A CHART

The navigator reads a chart in much the same way a soldier interprets a land survey map. The general shape of the seabed and the nature of the bottom are particularly important to fishermen. A good chart will have a high density of sounding and bottom information, but the technique of applying this to a particular fishing operation is perfected only with considerable experience.

In order to understand a chart, become very familiar with the symbols and abbreviations. These symbols are itemized and explained in *Chart No. 1** and should be studied in the initial stages of learning about chartwork.

Some Important Symbols

1. Exposed Rock; Elevation in Feet above Mean High Water

$\mathcal{O}$ (25).

2. Rock which Covers and Uncovers; in Feet above Chart Datum

$*$ (6)

3. Rock Awash at Chart Datum

$\ddag$

Note: When 2 or 3 is surrounded by a dotted circle, the rock is considered a danger to navigation.

4. Sunken Danger with Depth Swept by Wire Drag; in Feet or Fathoms

4 OBSTR.

5. Snags or Submerged Stumps

°₀ Snags

6. Foul Ground

(Foul)

7. Wreck, Part of which is Visible above Chart Datum

8. Sunken Wreck, Possibly Dangerous to Navigation

9. Sunken Wreck, not Dangerous to Navigation

10. Radio Direction Finding Station

⊙ R.D.F.

11. Radar Reflector

Ra Ref

12. Radar Responder Beacon

⊙ Racon.

13. R Starboard Hand Buoy "2" Entering from Seaward

R "2"

14. Port Hand Buoy "1" Entering from Seaward

"1"

Chart No. 1: United States of America Nautical Chart Symbols and Abbreviations (latest edition). Washington, D.C.: Department of Defense, Defense Mapping Agency, Hydrographic/Topographic Center.

Some Important Abbreviations

Lt. Ho.	Lighthouse	S.	Sand	wh.	White
Bn.	Light beacon	M.	Mud	bk.	Black
F.	Fixed light	St.	Stones	bu.	Blue
Occ.	*Occulting light	Rk.	Rocky	gn.	Green
Fl.	Flashing light	Sh.	Shells	yl.	Yellow
Qk. Fl.	Quick flashing light	Oys.	Oysters	rd.	Red
Gp. Fl.	Group flashing light	Ms.	Mussels	br.	Brown
OBSC.	Obscured light	Wd.	Seaweed	gy.	Gray

Note that all soundings are given in fathoms and/or feet at chart datum. Thus 11₄ would be a sounding of 11 fathoms and 4 feet at chart datum. Chart datum is most simply described as: *The level below which the tide seldom falls.* Chart datum is mean low water on the eastern seaboard of the United States.

Heights of land or conspicuous objects are given in feet above mean high water level unless otherwise stated in notes below the chart title. The depth contour lines as laid out in *Chart No. 1* should be noted.

Fishermen usually plot "snags" and "hangups" as they are encountered during fishing operations. Such obstructions are also often listed in a fishing logbook together with details of seasonal movement of fish species, water temperature, etc.

Exercise:
Chart Symbols (Charts 1, 13009, and 13205)

1. a. What is the meaning of the symbol at 40-57.8N, 072-07.9W?

    b. What is the meaning of the symbol bearing 177° T from Southeast Point Light, distance 5.0 miles?

    c. What is the meaning of the symbol where the Loran position line 9960-X-25830 crosses the 20-fathom curve and the Loran position line 9960-W-14517?

2. Fully describe the buoy at:
    a. 41-01.8N, 071-45.7W   d. 41-07.0N, 071-43.1W
    b. 41-15.5N, 071-34.6W   e. 41-20.9N, 071-34.6W
    c. 41-06.0N, 071-46.3W

3. Explain the reason why AREA B to the north of Gardiners Island is listed as a Danger Area.

4. Interpret the characteristics of the following lights:
    a. Point Judith   b. Watch Hill Pt.   c. Montauk Pt.

5. Explain the dashed magenta lines around Long Island.

6. What is the meaning of the quality of the bottom symbol nearest to the positions given in question 2, above?

7. Fully explain the use of the device shown at 40-48.6N, 067-40.0W.

8. Quote the explanation of green-tinted areas found on Chart 13009.

*Occulting light has a greater period of flash than darkness between flashes.

9. Sketch the symbols for submarine cables and cable areas found near Nebraska Shoal. What precautions should be taken when trawling in the vicinity of submarine cables and pipelines?

10. Fully describe the following lights:

    a. Highland   b. Cape Sable   c. Seal Island

5

GENERAL CHART LAYOUT

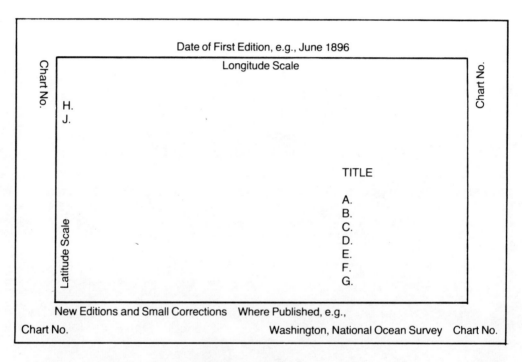

A. Type of projection used to transfer the curved section of surface area of the earth onto the flat surface of the chart, e.g., Mercator.

B. Scale of the chart, e.g., 1:80,000.

C. Sounding datum and whether depths are given in fathoms or feet, e.g., soundings in feet at mean low water (M.L.W.).

D. Level from which heights are given, e.g., heights in feet above mean high water (M.H.W.).

E. Cautions, hazards, and dangers to navigation; e.g., heavy tide rips may be experienced in a certain position at a given state of tide. These clauses must be well studied before using the chart.

F. An explanation of the tidal information contained on the chart, e.g., a series of vector diagrams superimposed on the chart showing tide strength and direction for each hour after high water (H.W.) at a given port.

G. A short summary of Loran or Decca navigator information available in the region.

H. Submarine cable and pipeline information and warnings.

J. Dumping grounds, firing or torpedo ranges, and protected fishing grounds.

Some of the warnings and cautions printed on the chart may refer to the *United States Coast Pilot* book for the region concerned. These pilot books give a highly detailed description of all factors relevant to the safe navigation of the zone covered and should be used in conjunction with the chart. Many interesting historical features are also related. Details about lights and beacons are contained in volumes of the *Light List*.

Note the date of a new edition as the accuracy of modern electronic surveying equipment improves the reliability of the chart.

Care should be taken when transferring a position from one chart to the next. The observed position should be checked as soon as possible on the new chart. The scale of the chart may differ greatly from the first one used, and it is important to double-check the distance scale used. For this reason it is advisable to have only one chart in use at a time.

Chart Construction

Prominent objects are positioned by extending a framework of angles and bearings from the known position of established points, called triangulation stations. Further detail is superimposed, and lines of soundings are run off. Position of wrecks, rocks, shoals, and all other important features are closely checked and rechecked. This information is presented on a field chart prior to final printing of the navigational chart.

6

DISTANCE

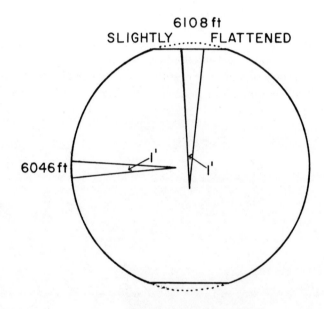

Nautical Mile, Knot

The nautical mile (n.m.) is the arc of a meridian subtended by an angle of 1' at the center of curvature of that section. As previously mentioned, the earth is slightly flattened at the poles. Therefore, the center of curvature in this region will be at a greater distance from the surface than it will be near the equator. This results in the distance subtended by 1' at the center of curvature being 6,108 feet at the poles and 6,046 feet at the equator. A mean of 6,076 feet is assumed for the International Nautical Mile, this being the value in about lat. 45° N and S.

It is common practice to divide the nautical mile into 10 equal parts which are called cables. For this purpose the length of a nautical mile is further approximated to 6,000 feet, thus giving the cable a value of 600 feet.

The unit of speed used at sea is the knot. One knot is 1 nautical mile travelled in 1 hour. This should not be confused with distance but is used purely as a unit to indicate speed.

Exercise:
True Course and Distance (Chart 13218)

1. Find the true course and distance from a position 41-10N, 071-30W to 41-20N, 071-00W.

2. Find the true course and distance from the tip of Sakonnet Pt. bearing due north at 3 miles to Gay Head Lt. bearing due east at 2 miles. How close to Buzzards Tower will you pass?

3. A vessel steers 200° T at 8 knots from Vineyard Sound Whistle Buoy. In what longitude will she cross the 20-fathom line to the south of Cox Ledge, and how long will this take?

4. A vessel fishing in 41-05N, 071-21.7W hauls up and proceeds to Point Judith at 9 knots. What true course should be made good, and how long will it take before she enters the gap in the East Breakwater?

5. A vessel leaves position 41-10N, 071-20W at 1800 hours steaming at 9½ knots. What course should be made good to the No. 26 Bell Buoy south of Nobska Pt., and what is the estimated time of arrival (E.T.A.)?

6. A fishing vessel passing close to Brenton Reef Tower hears of good catches being made near the 24-fathom patch to the north of Cox Ledge. How soon can she be there at 7 knots, and what course should be made good?

7. From the 24-fathom patch north of Cox Ledge, the vessel, slowed to 6 knots by a head wind, proceeds to Point Judith. What course should be made good, and how long will it take to reach the East Breakwater gap?

8. Find the true course and distance from where Southeast Pt. Lt. is 3 miles abeam to port to where Gay Head Lt. is 2 miles abeam to starboard. (To find abeam position draw distance circles from the point and lay off course line tangential to these circles. The abeam position will be where a perpendicular to the course line from the point intersects the course line.)

9. From a position with Cuttyhunk I. Lt. bearing 040° T and Gay Head Lt. bearing 088° T, find the true course and distance to the bell buoy at the entrance to Block I. Old Harbor.

10. From a position with Beavertail Pt. Lt. in range with Point Judith Lt. in 15 fathoms, find the true course and distance to where the Sakonnet River Whistle Buoy will be abeam to starboard, keeping Aband. Lt. Ho. Tower directly ahead.

7

THE RUNNING FIX

As previously stated, a single bearing gives only a position line somewhere along which the vessel must be situated. If a cross fix cannot be obtained, the "running fix" will give a reasonable determination of the vessel's position by advancing the initial bearing through a future dead-reckoning position and crossing this with another bearing of the same or another object at that time. This principle of the transferred position line is described below in four steps.

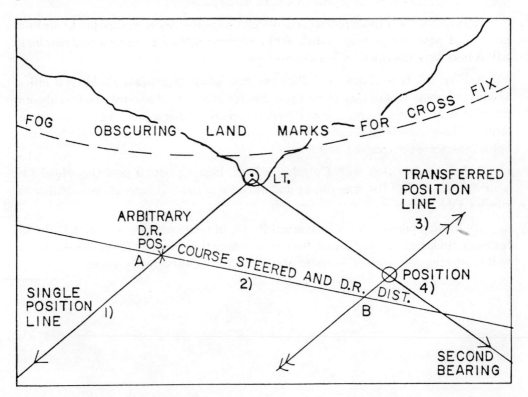

Principle of the Transferred Position Line

1. Lay off the first bearing.

2. Anywhere on this bearing mark an arbitrary dead-reckoning (D.R.) position A, and project course steered and D.R. distance AB.

3. Advance first bearing line so that it passes through point B (and has the same direction as in Step 1). It is reasonable to assume, providing course and distance AB are not in appreciable error, the vessel must now lie somewhere along this transferred position line.

4. At time of B, take a second bearing of the same or another object. The point where this bearing crosses the transferred position line will be a reasonably accurate determination of position known as a running fix.

It should be emphasized that the accuracy of the running fix depends on a correct determination of the run between bearings. The wind (or leeway) effect and current (or set and drift) effect can be allowed for as indicated in the diagram below.

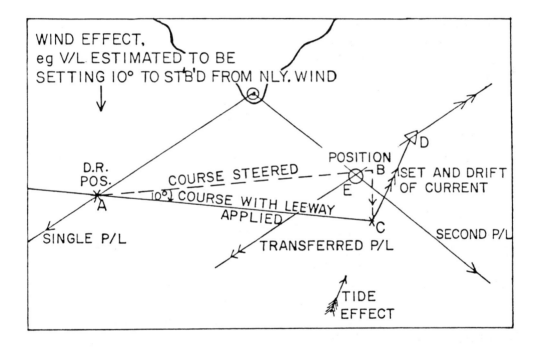

1. A is marked as D.R. position somewhere on first bearing and course steered AB is laid off.

2. In this case 10° of leeway is estimated for a northerly wind; this is shown as BC. Thus, AC is course with leeway applied.

3. The set, or direction of current, and drift, which is the distance the ship is affected by the current between bearings, is determined and applied as CD.

4. D is the point through which the transferred position line is drawn.

5. Where the second bearing intersects the transferred position line is the vessel's determined position, E. The second position line can be from any other source, e.g., Loran or radio direction finder.

In order to avoid confusion in the construction of the running fix, or any other chartwork for that matter, it is advisable to adopt a uniform set of symbols for practical use, as suggested below:

X D.R. Position

⚫ Single Position Line

△ Estimated Position

⚫ Transferred Position Line

☉ Observed Position (Fix) or
   Running Fix (R. Fix)

⚫ Set and Drift of Current

Exercise:
Running Fix (Chart 13218)

1. At 0600 Southeast Pt. Lt. bore 023° T, with the vessel in D.R. position 41-03N, 071-35W, steaming at 7 knots on a course of 070° T. At 0700 the same light was bearing 305° T. Find the vessel's position at 0700. What should the depth sounder indicate at this time?

2. The building at southeast point of Noman's Land bore 310° T to a vessel in D.R. position 41-05N, 070-36W, steering 243° T at 8 knots. One and a quarter hours later the same point bore due true north. Find the vessel's position at the time of the second bearing.

3. At 1030 Buzzards Tower bore 052° T to a vessel in D.R. position 41-22N, 071-05W, steaming 276° T at 12 knots. At 1115 Brenton Reef Tower bore 310° T. Find the position at this time.

4. At 1400 Gay Head Lt. bore 030° T to a ship in D.R. position 41-15N, 070-53W, steaming at 11 knots on a course of 297° T. Half an hour later Buzzards Tower was bearing 336° T. Find the position at 1430 and the true course to steer to Sakonnet River Whistle Buoy.

5. After passing the Vineyard Sound fairway buoy, at 1000 Loran ceased to operate with a final reading of 9960-W-14275. The vessel then proceeded at a reduced speed of 3 knots in fog, steering 055° T into Vineyard Sound. Nothing was seen until 1240 when Robinson's Hole bell buoy was observed 25° on the port bow. Find the position at this time by the transferred position line method.

6. A vessel proceeding NNW into Rhode Island Sound heading for the Vineyard Sound fairway buoy after fishing to the southward first crossed the 20-fathom curve at about 070-52W. Using this depth contour as a transferred position line, find the vessel's position one hour later when Gay Head Lt. was seen 4 points on the starboard bow, and the vessel was steaming at 8 knots. (Note that the compass card is divided into 32 points; 1 point = 11¼°.)

7. At 0400 Southeast Pt. Lt. was bearing 010° T, and the vessel in D.R. position 41-03N, 071-35W was steering 070° T at 8½ knots. Find the vessel's estimated position at 0500 when Southeast Pt. Lt. bore 282° T, if a current was estimated to be setting 030° T at 2½ knots.

8. At 1130 Point Judith Lt. was in range with No. 2 Whistle Buoy and the vessel in D.R. position 41-15N, 071-27W was steering 305° T at 6 knots. Find the position at

1230 if Point Judith Lt. bore 065° T, and a current was estimated to be setting NE at 2 knots.

9. At 1530 West I. near Sakonnet Pt. was bearing 322° T to a vessel in D.R. position 41-23N, 071-08W steaming at 7 knots with a course order to the helmsman of 290° T. A northerly wind was estimated to be giving 8° leeway and an ebb current was believed to be setting 140° T at 2 knots. Find the vessel's position at 1630 when Point Judith Lt. bore 249° T.

10. At 1900 Buzzards Tower bore 043° T to a vessel at Browns Ledge steaming 15 knots with a course order to the helmsman of 060° T, making an estimated 12° leeway for a strong north-northwesterly wind. A current was estimated to be setting 050° T at 2½ knots. Find the vessel's position at 1948 if Gay Head Lt. was bearing 170° T.

Note: Relative bearings are usually stated in degrees clockwise or to starboard of the ship's heading or may be specified as a given number of degrees to port or starboard of the ship's head as in question 5 above.

8

EARTH'S MAGNETISM

So far we have only been concerned with courses and bearings as laid down on the chart, that is, true courses and bearings related to the true, or geographical, north pole. Unfortunately, the north-seeking end of the magnetic compass needle does not seek the true north pole, but is attracted toward the magnetic north pole.

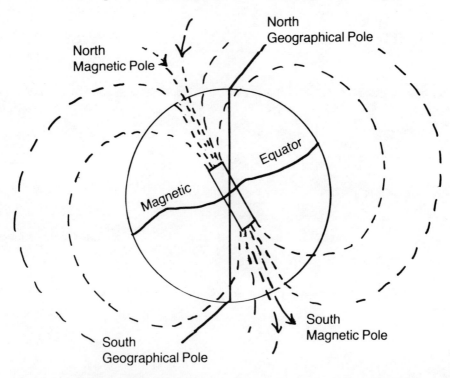

For all practical purposes the earth's magnetic effect can be likened to that of a bar magnet running along a diameter of the earth. The blue end of this magnet is situated somewhere beneath the northern Hudson Bay region and constitutes the north magnetic pole while the red end of the magnet is about 1,800 miles south of Tasmania to give the south magnetic pole.

The compass needle is merely a small, freely suspended bar magnet. Following the first basic law of magnetism, "opposite poles attract," it will attempt to align itself, red pole pointing toward magnetic north and blue pole toward magnetic south.

Magnetic Characteristics

The Magnetic Equator

About midway between the magnetic poles, there will be equal attraction of the blue end of the compass needle for the south magnetic pole and of the red end of the needle for the north magnetic pole. In this position the compass needle will lie horizontally. If the needle were moved toward a pole, its one end would be more strongly attracted than the other. It would dip out of the horizontal until the pole was reached and a maximum angle of dip of 90° would result. This feature renders the magnetic compass useless near either magnetic pole. The region surrounding earth (roughly midway between the magnetic poles) where there is no horizontal dip of a compass needle is known as the magnetic equator, or aclinic line.

Magnetic Meridian

A freely suspended compass needle, when subjected to the earth's magnetic influence alone, will line up with a meridian passing through the magnetic poles.

Variation

Variation is the angle between the true and magnetic meridians at the place considered. It is the number of degrees that the compass needle is deflected east or west of the true meridian due to the effect of earth's magnetism alone.

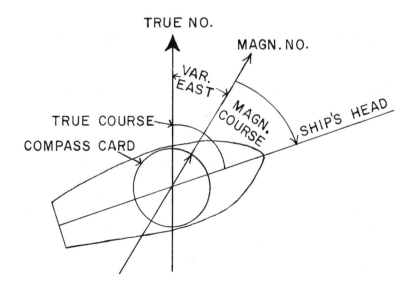

Note in the diagram that the compass card remains steady. The magnetic course is altered by applying helm and allowing the fore and aft lines to move around the compass card.

From the diagram it is easily seen that easterly variation will give a magnetic course smaller than the true course. It follows that westerly variation must be added to the true course to obtain the magnetic course.

Magnetic Direction

True Course

The true course is the angle between the true meridian passing through the vessel and the vessel's fore and aft line.

Magnetic Course

The magnetic course is the angle between the magnetic meridian passing through the vessel and the vessel's fore and aft line.

Secular Change

The positions of the magnetic poles change slightly each year so there is a consequent small change in the value of magnetic variation. This secular change is not a constant value and is itself subject to change. Therefore, when updating variation values by applying secular change from information printed on the compass roses of old charts, caution should be taken. If possible take the variation value for the area concerned from an up-to-date isogonic chart.

Isogonic Lines

Isogonic lines are lines passing through places having the same magnetic variation.

Agonic Line

Agonic line is the isogonic line representing zero variation.

Isallogonic Lines

Isallogonic lines are lines passing through places having the same secular change in variation.

Exercise:
Variation and Magnetic Course (Chart 13205)

1. True course and variation given, state magnetic course:
   a. 035° T, Var. 17° W   d. 348° T, Var. 15° E
   b. 097° T, Var. 12° E   e. 357° T, Var. 12° W
   c. 268° T, Var. 28° W

2. Magnetic bearing and variation given, state true bearing:
   a. 078° M, Var. 23° W   d. 356° M, Var. 14° E
   b. 143° M, Var. 16° E   e. 011° M, Var. 17° W
   c. 289° M, Var. 31° W

3. True and magnetic bearings given, state variation:

    a. 089° T, 058° M   d. 289° T, 298° M

    b. 158° T, 187° M   e. 357° T, 017° M

    c. 197° T, 164° M

4. Find the magnetic course from Southwest Ledge Bell Buoy to Cerberus Shoal Whistle Buoy.

5. Find the magnetic course from Gangway Rock Lighted Bell Buoy 2 to pass 3 miles off Montauk Pt. Lt. when abeam.

9

SHIP'S MAGNETISM

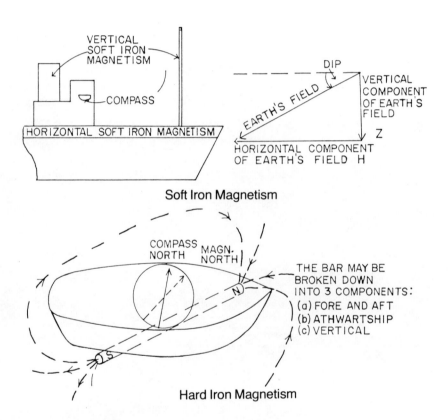

Soft Iron Magnetism

Hard Iron Magnetism

The effect of the earth's magnetic properties on the compass needle is complicated by the effects of magnetic fields set up by the iron contained in the ship itself. This text will not discuss in detail the various components of a ship's magnetic properties, but they may be broadly regarded in two groups: Permanent, or hard iron, magnetism induced into the ship's structure during building and variable, or soft iron, magnetism which varies according to the intensity of the component of the earth's field that induces it.

Deviation

Deviation is the amount that the compass needle is deflected from the magnetic meridian due to the effects of the ship's iron. It can be clearly seen from the preceding diagram that as the vessel alters course around the steady card its various magnetic poles will be presented at differing angles to the compass needle. Thus, deviation is not a constant error; its value changes with alteration of course.

Compass Correction

The ship's magnetic disturbing effects are compensated for as much as possible by placing correctors of equal and opposite effect near the compass. The basic principle observed in compass correction is: "Like cures like."

Fore and aft hard iron magnetism is compensated for by a fore and aft magnet of equal and opposite effect, and athwartship hard iron magnetism is opposed by an athwartship magnet of equal and opposite effect. The soft iron disturbing fields are compensated for by two athwartship soft iron balls and a vertical soft iron bar called the Flinder's bar, which is placed in the fore and aft line usually forward of the compass.

The process of compass correction is done by practical experiment. The ship is "swung" through 360° of the compass and steadied on various headings in order to note the deviation by observing the difference between the compass bearing of a distant object and its known magnetic bearing. These deviations are then reduced as much as possible by the compensation process, and any remaining deviations are observed and plotted in table form for practical use at sea. Examples of deviation tables and curves follow.

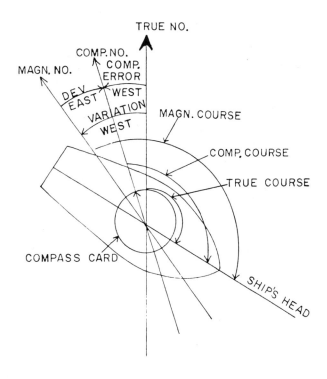

Compass Course and Compass Error

Compass course is the angle between compass north and the ship's head. Compass error is the amount that a compass needle is deflected out of the true meridian due to the combined effects of variation and deviation.

$$\text{Compass error} = \text{variation} \pm \text{deviation}$$

It can be seen from the above diagram that if variation and deviation are of opposite name they are to be subtracted to give the compass error. If variation and deviation are the same name they are added to give the compass error.

Also note from the same diagram that if the compass error is west then the compass course is greater than the true course. Similarly, if the deviation is west then the compass course is greater than the magnetic course.

Compass error, or deviation west, then compass course best
Compass error, or deviation east, then compass course least

Deviation Card I

Compass	Course	Deviation	Curve		Magnetic Course
N	000°	7° E	N		007°
NNE	022½°	7° E	NNE		029½°
NE	045°	6½° E	NE		051½°
ENE	067½°	6° E	ENE		073½°
E	090°	4° E	E		094°
ESE	112½°	2° E	ESE		114½°
SE	135°	1° W		SE	134°
SSE	157½°	4° W		SSE	153½°
S	180°	6° W		S	174°
SSW	202½°	7½° W		SSW	195°
SW	225°	7° W		SW	218°
WSW	247½°	6° W		WSW	241½°
W	270°	3½° W		W	266½°
WNW	292½°	Nil		WNW	292½°
NW	315°	4° E	NW		319°
NNW	337½°	6° E	NNW		343½°
N	000°	7° E	WEST	EAST	007°

Deviations for intermediate directions of the ship's head can be quickly calculated from the rate of change of deviation between the nearest known points, or it can be taken directly from the curve.

Example 1.

Find deviation for 256° C from Deviation Card I.

256° C is 8½° beyond WSW toward W where deviation changes 2½° in 22½° of course alteration

$$\text{Deviation on } 256°\,C = 6°\,W - \frac{8\frac{1}{2}}{22\frac{1}{2}} \times 2\frac{1}{2}$$

Deviation on 256° C = 6° W − .94° (deviation is decreasing)
For all practical purposes, deviation = 5° W

Example 2.

Find deviation for 130° from Deviation Card I.

130° C is 5° from SE back toward ESE where deviation changes 3° in 22½° of course alteration

$$\text{Deviation on } 130° \text{C} = 1°\text{W} - \frac{5}{22\frac{1}{2}} \times 3$$

Deviation on 130° C = 1° W − ⅔° (deviation is decreasing)
For all practical purposes, deviation = nil

In examples 1. and 2. we have found the deviation for a given compass course. Deviation is used more often in a reverse manner, being applied to a known magnetic course required to be steered between two given points.

Example 3.

A course of 125° T is required where variation is 18° W. Find the compass course to steer using Deviation Card I.

125° T with Var. 18° W gives 143° M
143° M lies between 134° M and 153½° M on Deviation Card I. In this region the deviation changes from 1° W to 4° W in 19½° magnetic. 143° is 9° beyond 134° with deviation increasing from 1° W.

$$\text{Deviation for } 143° \text{ M} = 1°\text{W} + \frac{9}{19\frac{1}{2}} \times 3$$

Deviation for 143° M = 1° W + 1.4° (deviation is increasing)
Deviation for 143° M = 2.4° W
Compass course to steer = 145½° C

In a nutshell, variation (the effect of the earth's magnetic properties) is applied to the true course to obtain the magnetic course, and deviation (the effect of the ship's magnetic properties) is applied to the magnetic course to obtain the compass course to steer.

Exercise:
Deviation, Compass Course, and Compass Error

Given the following information:

Compass Course	Deviation		Compass Course	Deviation
N	5W		S	1½E
NNE	5W		SSW	2½E
NE	5W		SW	3½E
ENE	4½W		WSW	3½E
E	4W		W	3E
ESE	3W		WNW	1½E
SE	2W		NW	1W
SSE	Nil		NNW	3W

1. Compile Deviation Card II together with curve of deviations to scale.

2. From Deviation Card II, find the deviation for the following compass courses, by both calculation and consulting the curve: 057° C, 129° C, 168° C, 239° C, 307° C.

3. Using Deviation Card II, find the deviation for the following magnetic courses: 038° M, 167° M, 232° M, 280° M, 307° M.

4. From Deviation Card I, find the deviation for the following compass courses: 079° C, 127° C, 174° C, 284° C, 307° C.

5. From Deviation Card I, find the deviation for the following magnetic courses: 089° M, 127° M, 188° M, 281° M, 331° M.

6. Fill in the blanks in this table.

	True Course	Variation	Magnetic Course	Deviation	Compass Error	Compass Course
a)	128°	28°W		3°E		
b)	207°			6°W	24°W	
c)		18°E	256°	3°W		
d)			306°	7°E	22°W	
e)		21°E			17°E	016°
f)		18°W		5°W		337°
g)	196°		174°			181°
h)				2°E	2°W	010°
i)	232°	27°E			30°E	
j)		18°W	154°		14°W	
k)	352°			6°W	37°E	
l)		19°E	218°			223°
m)		36°W			25°W	176°
n)				9°E	14°W	256°
o)	018°		357°			000°
p)	359°			1°E	18°W	
q)		24°E	295°	6°W		
r)	006°		347°	11°E		
s)	001°	11°E		11°W		
t)		27°W			14°E	346°

10

THE COMPASS

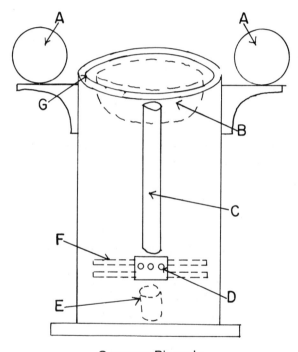

Compass Binnacle

Key to Compass Binnacle

A. Athwartship soft iron correctors

B. Compass bowl (painted white with black fore and aft lubber line to steer by)

C. Flinder's bar, fore and aft soft iron corrector

D. Fore and aft permanent corrector magnets

E. Bucket which contains vertical corrector magnets and which also helps to correct for disturbing forces created when ship heels

F. Athwartship permanent correct magnets

G. Gimbals and antivibrational springs and mountings

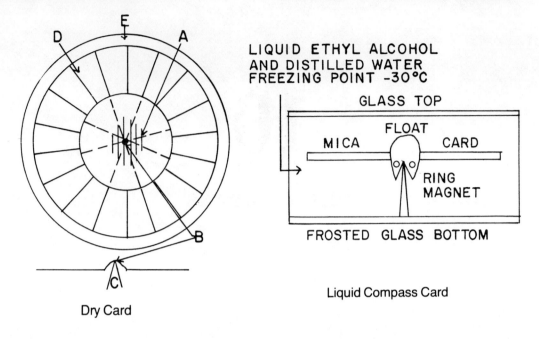

LIQUID ETHYL ALCOHOL
AND DISTILLED WATER
FREEZING POINT -30°C

Liquid Compass Card

Dry Card

Key to Dry Card

A. Set of needle magnets of cobalt steel held in place by silk threads
B. Center sapphire jeweled bearing
C. Iridium pivot
D. Card made in sections of rice paper to allow for any expansion or contraction
E. Aluminum outer ring

Note on Liquid Compass Card

In general the liquid card is much more stable than the dry card because the liquid quickly "damps out" oscillations of the card due to motion of the ship. Such a "dead beat" type of compass is generally preferred

The Gyro Compass

The gyro compass consists of a heavy wheel, called the rotor, which is rotated at high speed by an electric motor. The property of gyroscopic inertia in a spinning gyro allows the axis to remain rigid in its direction no matter how its supporting frame is moved. This principle is utilized by applying a gravity control to the axis, causing it to oscillate about the true meridian. The oscillation is further controlled by a damping system which causes the axis to settle, usually within 1° of the true meridian. The danger of incorrect application of variation, deviation, or both is removed.

Modern gyro compasses are sturdy, compact, and efficient and lend themselves well to such refinements as automatic helmsman and course-stabilized radar display. However, the cost of such equipment is beyond the means of many smaller boat operators.

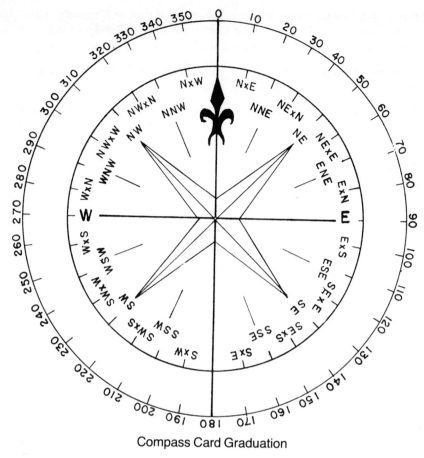

Compass Card Graduation

When converting from one notation to the other, remember 1 point = 11¼°.

Exercise:
Compass Courses and Bearings (Chart 13205)

1. Using Deviation Card I and variation from the compass rose, find the position of a vessel steering 020° C when Southeast Pt. Lt. was bearing 035° C and Montauk Pt. Lt. was bearing 312° C.

2. The Tall Building south of Fort Pond bore 041° C, and East Hampton Spire bore 297° C. Find the vessel's position using Deviation Card II if she was steering 145° C.

3. Watch Hill Pt. was bearing due north by compass while Race Pt. was bearing 308° C. Find the position if the vessel was steering 072° C, using Deviation Card I.

4. The Stone Tower on Beacon Hill was in range with the Aeronautical Lt. on Block Island on a bearing of 143½° C. By determination of the true direction of their range, calculate the deviation of the vessel's compass. If, at this same time, on the same heading, Sandy Pt. Lt. bore 062½° C, how far off the land is this vessel?

5. The vessel was steering 142° C and, using Deviation Card I, Race Pt. Lt. bore 306° C while the depth sounder recorded 30 fathoms. What should the compass bearing of Little Gull I. Lt. have been at this time?

6. Point Judith west breakwater lights were in line bearing due north compass. Find the deviation of the compass at that time and, if Sandy Pt. Lt. was bearing 250° C, how many miles off the east breakwater entrance was the vessel?

7. Find the compass course to steer from Gardiners Pt. Bell Buoy to pass 1 mile to the northward of Shagwong Reef Buoy. Use Deviation Card II.

8. Find the compass course and distance from a position 4 cables* southwest of Race Pt. Lt. to the No. 3 Gong Buoy off Montauk Pt. Also find the compass course necessary to steer due south true from the gong buoy. Use Deviation Card I.

9. Montauk Pt. Lt. bore 032° C to a vessel steering 048° C at 9 knots. One hour later the same light was bearing 354° C. Using Deviation Card I, find the vessel's position at the time of the second bearing.

10. At 0630 Watch Hill Pt. Lt. was bearing 322° C to a vessel steaming 254° C at 7½ knots. A northerly wind was giving the vessel an estimated 5° leeway, and the current was estimated to be setting 030° T at 2 knots. Find the vessel's position at 0730 if Watch Hill Pt. Lt. was then bearing 042° C. Use Deviation Card II. What compass course should now be steered to pass through "The Race" 4 cables off Race Pt. Lt.?

*One cable is 0.1 of a nautical mile.

11

CHART PROJECTIONS

There are numerous methods used for transferring all or part of the surface of a
sphere onto a plane surface. A section of a sphere cannot be flattened out without
distortion. Because of this "undevelopable" property, either a cylinder, a cone, or a
tangential plane is used to represent the section. These are developable surfaces in
that they can be flattened into chart form without distortion.

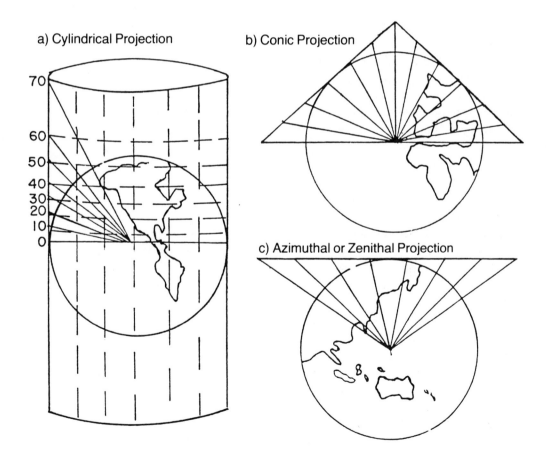

a) Cylindrical Projection

b) Conic Projection

c) Azimuthal or Zenithal Projection

A discussion of one of each of these projections and its importance in the production of charts follows. Any projection will have some degree of proportion, scale, or angular distortion, but in some cases this feature of a projection can be used to the navigator's advantage.

The Mercator Projection

The projection most favored and used to produce a great majority of charts is the Mercator projection which is effected by projecting from the center of the earth through certain positions on the earth's surface onto the inner surface of a circumscribing cylinder. It can be easily visualized that meridians of longitude will thus be represented as parallel straight lines. However, we know that on the globe they converge to meet at the poles. That is, 1' of longitude, which equals approximately 1' of latitude at the equator, gradually decreases to zero value at the poles. Thus we can say that the distance value of 1' of longitude varies with the cosine of the latitude concerned. On the Mercator projection we have removed this convergency of the meridians; therefore, theoretically we have cancelled the cosine value with secant value;

$$\text{Distance value of Long.} = \text{Long.} \times \text{cosine of Lat.} \times \frac{1}{\text{cosine of Lat.}}$$

In order to keep the area represented in the correct relative proportion it is also necessary to increase the distance between parallels of latitude by the same proportion, i.e., by the secant of the mean latitude. For this reason Mercator charts are of no value in the polar regions, the natural secant of 90° being infinity. Also, this is why it is important to measure distance on the latitude scale of the chart only in the immediate latitude concerned. The distance value, in nautical miles, for any given difference of longitude in a given latitude is known as *departure*.

The Gnomonic Projection

The gnomonic projection is a zenithal projection which is of particular value for portraying the polar regions. For a polar gnomonic chart the pole itself is the point of tangency of the plane, and points on the earth's surface are projected onto its underside by means of straight lines from the center of the earth. Meridians of longitude will therefore appear as spokes from the center and parallels of latitude, as concentric circles. The gnomonic chart is also commonly called a great circle chart because straight lines laid off on such a chart will be great circles.

This property allows a relatively inexperienced navigator to take advantage of great circle sailing without going through the more difficult calculations necessitated by the mathematical approach to it. While a straight line is the shortest distance between two points on a plane surface, the arc of a great circle is the shortest distance between two points on the surface of a sphere. A straight line tracked out by a vessel steering a steady course on the earth's surface will result in a spiral or loxodromic curve which cuts all meridians at the same angle. Such a curve is commonly called a *rhumb line*.

Note that a rhumb line appears as a straight line on a Mercator chart but will be a curve on a gnomonic chart while the converse will apply to a great circle.

A considerable distance can be saved by sailing a great circle track instead of a straight rhumb-line course on long ocean passages. This is easily accomplished by transferring so many positions through which a straight line on a gnomonic chart passes onto a Mercator chart of the same region. The interval of these positions is usually approximately a day or a half-day of normal steaming distance and the positions are joined by a series of straight rhumb lines which combine to give the nearest practical approximation to a great circle.

The Polyconic Projection

The simple conic projection is only accurate near the latitude of tangency of the cone. Considerable distortion will result at appreciable distances from this standard parallel. This fault can be overcome by the use of a series of cones (so that each latitude is the base of a tangent cone) and because many, or "poly," cones are used, the projection is termed polyconic. Parallels of latitude appear as nonconcentric circles, and meridians are curved slightly concave toward a central, straight meridian. The scale is true along the central meridian and any parallel of latitude. This type of projection is used extensively for maps of large land areas because a number of small maps are easily fitted into a large coverage. For this reason charts produced from this projection are sometimes used in navigating lakes or inland waterways.

12

PRACTICAL CHARTWORK

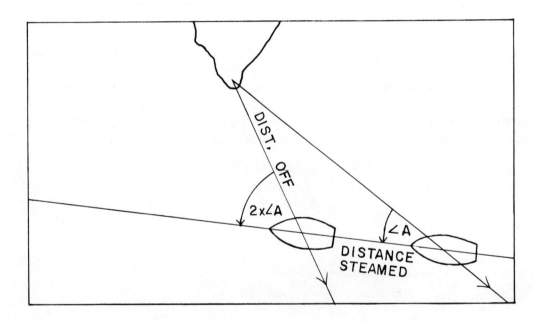

Mathematical Solutions to the Running Fix

A. Doubling the Angle on the Bow

If the angle between the ship's head and an object ashore is doubled by steaming a certain distance, then, because the exterior angle of a triangle is equal to the two interior opposite angles, the interior angles are equal. In other words, an isosceles triangle has been formed and the sides opposite the equal angles must also be equal. Therefore:

Distance steamed = distance off at second bearing

Any appreciable set and drift of current will render this method of fixing inaccurate. Also error is likely if very small angles are used.

B. The Four-Point Problem

A convenient application of doubling the angle on the bow, which serves as a good practical method of approximating position in small craft, uses the four-point bearing. A steady course is steered and the bearing of a shore mark is observed until it is four points (45°) on the bow. The vessel continues on a steady course and speed until the mark is abeam. Then the distance off abeam will be the distance steamed between the four-point bearing and the beam bearing. It is handy to have a small paint mark on the gunwale on each side of the bow at four points to the helmsman. These marks can be set up accurately while the vessel is alongside. It is important to have a good idea of the vessel's speed through the water for any type of running fix; perhaps, the best way of determining this is from a patent log. The log gear consists of a rotator which is towed behind the vessel and is attached by a log line to a critically geared clock which is graduated in nautical miles. The accuracy of the log can be improved by adjusting the length of log line until the distance recorded on the clock corresponds to that determined by fixed observations. Various, more sophisticated logs, more permanent in nature, are available, but are more expensive. One of these relies on the amount of power recorded by a small generator activated by a tiny propeller projecting beneath the hull. The amount of power depends on the revolutions of the propeller which, in turn, vary directly according to the vessel's speed relative to the water. Other logs rely on the pressure of water on a tube or tubes extending from the hull. Electromagnetic and Doppler logs also have come into general, widespread use.

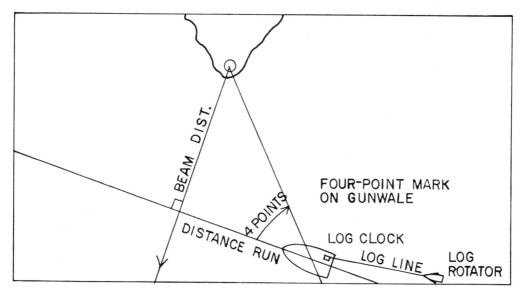

The distance run between an angle on the bow of 63½° and the four-point bearing will give half the distance off when abeam.

C. Distance Off Abeam Equals the Distance Run between Set Bearings

If the relative bearing of a shore object is increased as indicated in this table, then the distance run between the two bearings will be the distance off the object when it is abeam.

Relative bearings in degrees from ship's head	
22°	- 34°
25°	- 41°
26½°	- 45°
32°	- 59°
35°	- 67°
37°	- 72°

Leading and Clearing Marks

Leading and clearing marks, which may be natural or man-made, are extremely useful aids to chartwork when handling a ship in confined waters. Many helpful clearing and leading marks, which are not marked on the chart, can be discovered as the navigator gradually acquires local knowledge of a particular area. Various church towers, rocks, taverns, etc., when kept in line with a more conventional navigation mark, such as a buoy, beacon, or lighthouse, lead the vessel clear of rocks, shoals, and dangers.

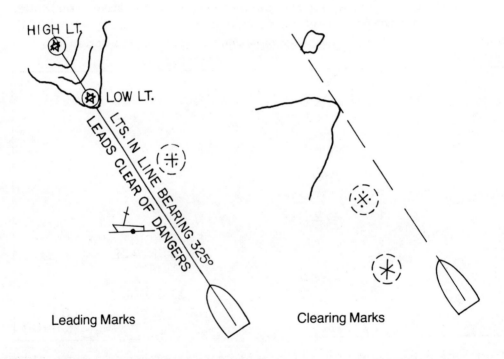

Leading Marks   Clearing Marks

Exercise:
Doubling the Angle on the Bow (Chart 13218)

1. A vessel steering due true north at 11 knots observed Gay Head Lt. bearing northeast. What distance will she be off the light when it is abeam some 22 minutes later?

2. A vessel steering 326° C observed Buzzards Tower four points on the starboard bow with the log reading 36. Give the latitude and longitude of the beam position if the log was reading 41.3 at this time. Use Deviation Card I.

3. A vessel steering 214° C sights the No. 2 Whistle Buoy to the south of Noman's Land 30° on the port bow with the log reading 97½. Some time later the buoy is 60° on the port bow and the log reads 101. Find the distance off at the time of the second bearing and also the distance off abeam. Use Deviation Card I.

4. A vessel steering 202° C sights Southeast Pt. Lt. 27° on the starboard bow. Some time later Southeast Pt. Lt. bears 256° C. If the total number of engine revolutions made between bearings indicated that the vessel had travelled 5 miles, give the vessel's position at the time of the second bearing. Use Deviation Card I.

5. Brenton Reef Tower was 35° on the starboard bow of a vessel steering 316° C with the log reading 47. When the log was reading 49 the Brenton Reef Tower was found to be 67° on the starboard bow. How far will the vessel be from Brenton Reef Tower when it is abeam if the present course and speed are maintained?

FIRST GENERAL CHARTWORK EXERCISE
(CHARTS 13009 AND 13218)

Use Deviation Card I, and assume that you are the skipper of a trawler fishing out of New Bedford in the Gulf of Maine area working as far east as Liverpool, Nova Scotia.

1. List the charts you will require on board. State what you should look for when checking these charts and list the allied publications you should have on board.

2. You pass through the New Bedford outer breakwater (hurricane barrier) at 0400 Monday morning and proceed at 6 knots on various courses until you reach No. 3 Gong Buoy at Negro Ledge. Here you increase speed to 9 knots and change course down Buzzards Bay for the Vineyard Sound Junction Lighted Whistle Buoy VS. What is this compass course and what is the least depth to be encountered on this track?

3. At Buoy VS the log reads 0432.10 and you change course to pass 2 cables offshore from Nomans Land Lighted Whistle Buoy 2.* What is this course?

4. A little later, with the log reading 0435.80, Gay Head Lt. had a compass bearing of 094 and, even later, with the log reading 0440.25, the same light was bearing 040. What is the position of this running fix?

5. From this position you change course to the same destination allowing 5° leeway for a westerly wind. What is this compass course?

6. At 0730, with the log reading 0444.60, Nomans Land Lighted Whistle Buoy 2 is abeam to port, 1 cable off. Transfer this position from Chart 13218 to Chart 13009. What is this position?†

7. At this position change course to head for Boston Approach Lighted Whistle Buoy BA. What is this compass course?

---

*Navigation Regulations prohibit all vessels from entering the PROHIBITED AREA between 01 NOV and 30 APR. These Regulations are to be found in the *U.S. Coast Pilot* (Volumes 1 and 2), which should be in your list for question 1, above.

†When shifting from one chart to another, the surest way to avoid position error is to use latitude/longitude values and not to use aids to navigation, particularly floating aids which might not be charted in the correct position. *With regard to this exercise, make sure that all aids are charted as for 1982 as shown on p. 11.*

8. Some time later, with the log reading 0492.50, Fishing Buoy 6 is close aboard to port. Even later, with the log reading 0525.00, BA Buoy is observed four points on the port bow. Then, with the log reading 0530.00, BA Buoy is abeam to port. What is the position of this running fix and what was the true course made good since leaving Fishing Buoy 6?

9. You continue on this same track until you reach the 40-fathom curve (at about 2000). Here you change course due east magnetic to begin trawling at an average speed of 2½ knots. Trawling continues at this average speed in this general direction for a full 24 hours. At the end of this time you have made a good catch and set course for Boston. The best knowledge you have of your position here is from dead reckoning and a sounding of 50 fathoms. What is the compass course to Boston Approach Lighted Whistle Buoy BD?

10. From Boston Approach Lighted Whistle Buoy BD, what is the compass course to Boston Approach Lighted Buoy BF?

11. With 17 Miles between the BF buoy and Commercial Wharf in Boston, what is your estimated time of arrival on Wednesday if you average a speed of 10 knots?

13

ALLOWING FOR WIND AND CURRENT

A current setting directly ahead or astern of a vessel will only affect the speed made good through the water and will not cause the vessel to be set from her course line. If the current is setting at any angle to the projected course line, it is necessary to alter course toward the current in order to make the course good. The amount of alteration obviously must vary according to the strength and relative direction of the current as well as the speed of the ship.

It is first necessary to estimate the set and rate of the current and allow for this as indicated in the following diagram. Any wind effect can be allowed for after this is done. Using the illustration below:

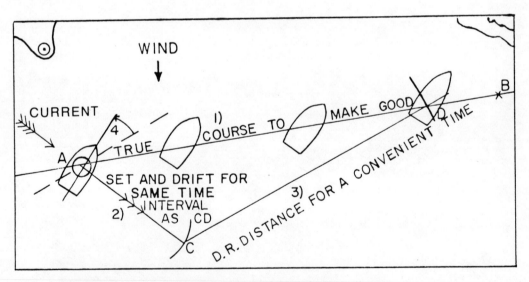

1. Lay off the course required to be made good, AB.

2. From A also lay off the estimated set and drift of current for any convenient time, usually 1 hour or 2 hours, AC.

3. With center C and radius equal to the D.R. distance for this convenient time, cut off CD on the line AB. Then CD is the course to steer to combat the current, and

AD is the distance made good. If AD is greater than CD, the current is said to be favorable. Otherwise, it is unfavorable.

4. Finally, leeway is counteracted by altering course into the wind. The amount of compensation for a given force of wind varies considerably for different conditions of draught and trim for one particular vessel. The accuracy of estimation of leeway improves with experience.

A helpful fact is that a 1° set to port or starboard of the course steered will give an error of about 100 feet in a distance of 1 mile run.

Exercise:
Allowing for Wind and Current (Chart 13009)

Use Deviation Card I throughout.

1. Find the compass course to steer from Nomans Land Lighted Whistle Buoy 2 to Davis South Shoal Lighted Whistle Buoy 8 DS in order to combat a current setting north at 2 knots if the vessel is steaming at 10 knots. What speed will the vessel make good? (Four to five hours is probably the best time factor to use in this case.)

2. Find the compass course to steer from Brazil Rock Lighted Whistle Buoy to Gull Rock Lighted Whistle Buoy to counteract a current setting 260° T at 3 knots. What speed will the vessel make good if her D.R. speed is 11 knots?

3. Give the compass course to steer from 42-45N, 067-00W to Boston Approach Lighted Buoy BB in order to combat a 2½-knot current setting from the south. If the vessel is steaming at 9 knots what speed should she make good?

4. Find the compass course to steer from 42-05N, 069-07W to a position 1 mile south of Eastern Pt. Lt. at the approaches to Gloucester. The current is estimated to be setting 300° T at 2 knots and 5° leeway is to be allowed for a southwesterly wind. The vessel has a D.R. speed of 12 knots.

5. Give the compass course and speed made good for a vessel steaming at 10 knots from Nomans Land Lighted Whistle Buoy 2 to Davis South Shoal Lighted Whistle Buoy and counteracting a current setting 050° T at 2½ knots. Leeway of 9° is to be allowed for a northerly wind.

6. A vessel 1 mile to the east of Pollock Rip Entrance Lighted Horn Buoy PR has the destination 41-40N, 068-00W. What compass course should she steer to counteract a current setting 340° T at 2 knots and a northerly wind estimated to be giving 8° leeway? The vessel has a steaming speed of 8 knots.

7. A vessel wishes to make good a course from Gannet Rock Lighted Bell Buoy 70Y to 42-10N, 065-18W. The mean time of the passage will be 8 hours after the time of maximum flood at Pollock Rip Channel. Using the current diagram in 42-50N, 065-56W, find the compass course to steer and the speed made good if the vessel is steaming at 7 knots.

8. Using the current diagram in 43-16N, 066-00W, find the compass course to steer from 42-35N, 065-22 W to pass 1 mile to the eastward of Lurcher Shoal Lighted

Whistle Buoy LURCHER. The mean time of passage is the time of maximum flood at Pollock Rip Channel, and the vessel is steaming at 11 knots. How long will it take before LURCHER is abeam?

9. A vessel leaves 40-54N, 067-47W with 41-40N, 068-12W as her destination. Find the compass course to steer to combat the current indicated by the vector near Cultivator Shoal for 8 hours after time of maximum flood at Pollock Rip Channel for the full moon period. Also allow 10° leeway for a westerly wind. If the vessel is steaming at 8 knots what speed will she make good?

10. A vessel steaming at 10 knots leaves 41-15N, 068-55 W with the current at maximum flood and the moon at first quarter. What compass course should be steered to make the Great Rip Lighted Buoy 4 allowing 10° for a southerly wind?

SECOND GENERAL CHARTWORK
EXERCISE (CHART 13218)

Use Deviation Card I and assume your vessel's steaming speed is 10 knots and her trawling speed is 3 knots unless otherwise shown.

1. You leave Point Judith East Breakwater Entrance at 0400 to fish within the 25-fathom "deep hole" 12 miles east of Block I. You intend to begin trawling where the 9960-W-14400 Loran line crosses the 25-fathom curve. With an average estimated current setting 350° at a speed of 2 knots and a southerly wind giving 5° leeway, what is this compass course to steer?

2. You do arrive at or close to your destination at the expected time and then you make two 2-hour drags toward the 30-fathom patch in the southwest leg of "deep hole," taking about 20 minutes between drags and keeping to this track as much as is possible so as to avoid known snags on each side. At 1012 the 25-fathom curve is crossed with the depth shoaling and a Loran reading of 9960-Y-43817.5. From this position a compass course of 005° is steered at 10 knots for 30 minutes. At the end of this time Southeast Pt. Lt. has a compass bearing of 291 at a distance of 6.7 miles by radar. What was the set and drift (speed) from 1012 to 1042 if the wind was calm?

3. At 1045 you begin a 1½-hour drag allowing 5° leeway for a southeast wind. What compass course should you steer so as to make good a course of 354 true, assuming the set and drift of the current remains the same as it was from 1012 to 1042? What distance over the bottom would you expect this drag to cover in the 1½ hours?

4. At 1200 a hurricane warning is received and you set course for the beginning of the inbound Buzzards Bay traffic lane, steering a compass course of 100. At 1230 you change your compass course to 046 and at 1400, with the Loran out of order and fog closed in, a radio direction finder *relative* bearing of 030 is taken on Buzzards Tower. At 1430 the radio direction finder *relative* bearing on Buzzards Tower is 130. What is your estimated position at 1430 if the current was setting 210° at 1½ knots during the previous 30 minutes?

5. What are the two compass courses from the 1430 estimated position to the hurricane barrier at New Bedford, altering course at the flashing green buoy just south of Negro Ledge? What is your estimated time of arrival at the hurricane barrier if, because of the fog, you reduce speed to 8½ knots at 1430?

14

TIDES

The combined gravitational effects of the moon and sun, in the power ratio of 7 to 3 respectively, attract the water envelope around 73 percent of the earth's surface into an elliptical shape. At spring tides their combined effects act together to give a very high, high water and a very low, low water, whereas at neap tides their effects are opposed which results in lower high waters and higher low waters. This simply means that the spring range of tide is far greater than the neap range. Spring tides occur in reciprocal longitudes at the time of new moon and full moon. As the earth rotates on its axis once each day, a given location will have two high and two low tides in about a day.

Spring Tides

The moon orbits the earth once every 29½ days, and the earth rotates on its axis each 23 hours 56 minutes 4 seconds. These two factors result in the moon crossing the observer's meridian every 24 hours 50 minutes. Because a high water also occurs when the moon is on the farther side of the earth, successive high waters will be about 12 hours 25 minutes apart, and the *duration of high water to low water* will be about 6 hours 12 minutes.

The tides for a certain port can be predicted by formulating the various tidal affecting forces into equations of tidal constants. These harmonic constants include the effects of the relative positions of the earth, moon, and sun and such modifying factors as the geographical layout of the port, shallow water effects, etc. The predic-

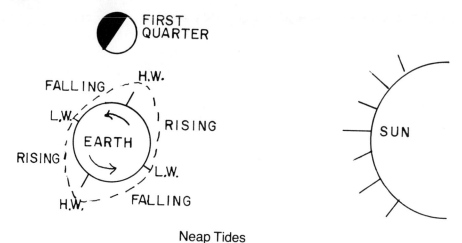

Neap Tides

tions of the time and height of low water and high water for one complete year for certain selected standard ports are contained in *Tide Tables*. Four volumes of these include tidal predictions for most of the major ports of the world. It is impractical to include every minor inlet and bay; such secondary places are referred, by a time and height difference, to the nearest standard port. A standard port may have ten to twenty secondary ports linked to it as indicated in a tidal difference table found toward the end of the tide tables.

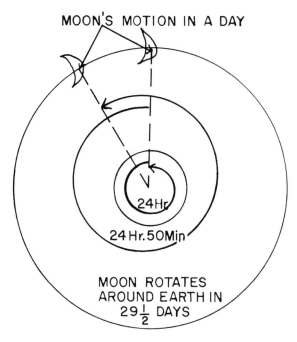

The tide tables state the expected time and height of high water and low water, but often it is necessary to know the height of the tide at an intermediate time or the time that the tide will attain a certain height. These problems are solved by the use of a table called the Height of Tide at Any Time. This table is designed under the assumption that vertical tidal motion is directly related to a cosine curve. However, this assumption is in most cases not strictly true and, therefore, data computed in this manner should be regarded as approximate only. A full explanation of the use of this table is contained in the tide table itself. Note that interpolation is not needed when using this table.

Remember always that the times and heights of tides contained in tide tables are computed from the past tidal history of the place and geographical, celestial, and average meteorological conditions. Unusual meteorological conditions, such as very low atmospheric pressure, a strong steady wind for a number of days, or a hurricane over a thousand miles away, can greatly distort the calculated tidal predictions. However, the tide tables are, in normal conditions, exceedingly accurate.

The times of H.W. and L.W. stated in the tables are for the time zone indicated by the standard meridian given. Thus, 75° W will be + 5 hours zone time because 15° = 1 hour, and 5 hours are to be added to obtain Greenwich mean time.

Daylight saving time, or summer time, should be applied afterwards.

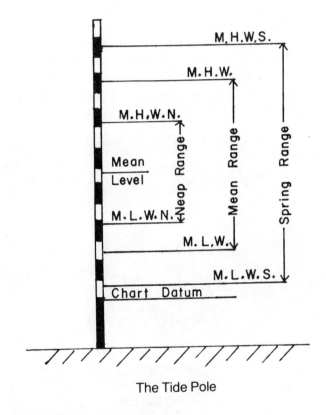

The Tide Pole

Exercise:
Tides (*East Coast America Tide Tables*)

1. Give the duration and range of ebb tide at Boston, Mass., on April 18 P.M.

2. State the duration and range of the A.M. flood tide at Newport, R.I., on Sept. 9.

3. Give the times and heights of H.W. and L.W. on the morning of July 15 at Wickford, R.I.

4. State the duration and range of flood tide at Block I. Harbor, R.I., on the evening of Feb. 18.

5. Give the times and heights of H.W. and L.W. for the morning of Aug. 22 at Catskill, N.Y.

6. Calculate the height of tide at New London, Conn., at 1800 on May 27.

7. Find the height of tide at Newport, R.I., at 0430 S.T. on June 10.

8. Calculate the time that the tide reaches a height of 7 feet on the morning of Dec. 29 at Boston, Mass.

9. Find the height of tide at Narragansett Pier, R.I., at 1530 on Jan. 17.

10. Between what times will there be less than 1 foot of tide at Point Judith, R.I., on Christmas morning?

Note that answers are given for 1968 tidal information. If the 1968 Tide Tables are not available, work the problems for any year, and disregard answers in the back of this book.

15

THE MARINE SEXTANT

The principal tool of trade of the "deep sea" navigator is the marine sextant. The sextant's main purpose is to measure the altitude of heavenly bodies above the visible horizon in order to compute the vessel's position.

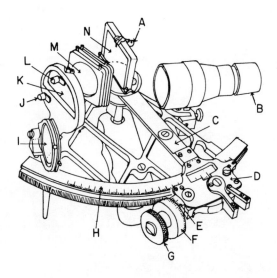

A Perpendicularity Adjustment Screw
B Telescope
C Index Bar
D Arc Clamp
E Vernier
F Micrometer
G Adjusting Wheel
H Graduated Arc
I Shades
J Parallelism Adjusting Screw
K Horizon Glass
L Side Error Adjustment Screw
M Shades
N Index Mirror

The sextant consists of a framework bearing a radial index bar. One end of the bar moves along a graduated arc, and the other end pivots about the center of curvature of the arc. The telescope is in line with the horizon glass which is in two halves. The half nearest the plane of the instrument is a plane mirror which shows the double reflection of an object from the index mirror. The other half is clear to allow the observer to look directly at an object. Thus, the reflected image of one object can be brought into line with another object by moving the index bar along the arc.

The sextant arc is about one-sixth of a circle but because the process of double reflection will result in a measured angle of only half the size of the true angle, the arc is graduated to about 120°. This second principle of the sextant is explained in the labelled diagram.

A micrometer allows readings to an accuracy of 1 minute of arc, and a small vernier attached to the micrometer facilitates readings down to 10 seconds of arc.

Principles

First Principle

When a ray of light strikes a plane mirror, the angle of incidence is always equal to the angle of reflection.

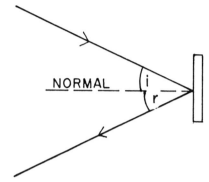

Second Principle

When a ray of light suffers two successive reflections in the same plane by two plane mirrors, the angle between the first and last rays is equal to twice the angle between the two mirrors.

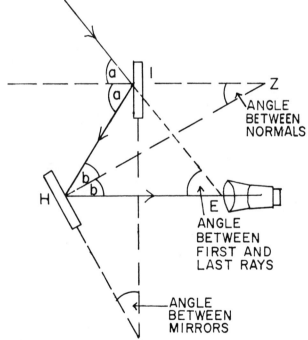

Note that the angle between the mirrors equals the angle between the normals to those mirrors (angle Z).

Proof

In triangle HIZ, exterior angle a = 2 interior opposite angles b + Z .... 1.
In triangle HIE, exterior angle 2a = 2b + E .... 2.
Multiply equation 1. by 2. Then 2a = 2b + 2Z
therefore 2b + E = 2b + 2Z
or, the angle between first and last rays (E) equals twice the angle between the mirrors (Z).

Errors and Adjustments

There are three main errors which are liable to exist in a sextant. These can be corrected by turning the appropriate adjustment screw.

1. Perpendicularity

The first error of the sextant is caused by the index glass not being truly perpendicular to the plane of the instrument. This error can be recognized by holding the sextant horizontally at arm's length. With the arc away from the observer and set at about 35°, the observer looks down into the index glass at a fine angle. If the reflection of the arc does not coincide with the arc itself, the error of perpendicularity exists. This error is corrected by turning the first adjustment screw on the back of the index mirror until the arc and its reflection do coincide.

2. Side Error

Side error of the sextant is due to the horizon glass not being truly perpendicular to the plane of the sextant. This error is found by holding the sextant obliquely with the arc at zero and observing the true and reflected images of a clear horizon. If the object and its image are not in a continuous line, side error exists. This error can also be found by rotating the micrometer screw back and forth each side of zero while looking at a star. If the reflected star does not pass directly over the true star, then side error exists. This error is corrected by turning the second adjustment screw on the back of the horizon glass until coincidence is effected.

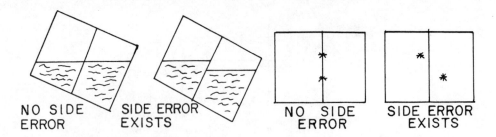

NO SIDE ERROR   SIDE ERROR EXISTS   NO SIDE ERROR   SIDE ERROR EXISTS

3. Error of Parallelism

The third adjustable error of the sextant, the error of parallelism, is caused by the index mirror and horizon glass not being truly parallel when the arc is set at zero. This error is discovered by setting the arc at zero and observing a clear horizon or a star which is not too bright with the sextant held vertically. If the true object and its reflected image do not coincide, then the error of parallelism exists. This error can be corrected by turning the third adjustment screw which is situated on the back of the horizon glass nearest to the plane of the instrument.

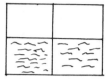

NO ERROR OF
PARALLELISM

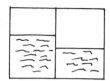

ERROR OF
PARALLELISM

Index Error

Side error and the error of parallelism are interrelated in that the correction of one error may induce the other. Adjustment for these two errors should be made alternately a number of times. Any error of parallelism remaining which cannot be removed without inducing side error is called index error. The index error must then be applied to every angle that is taken. When a larger arc reading than the true angle results, the index error is subtracted and termed "on the arc." When the sextant gives a smaller angle than the true angle, then obviously the index error is to be added and is termed so many minutes "off the arc." Index error is often zero and usually no more than 2 minutes or 3 minutes plus or minus.

Four Unadjustable Errors

There are four errors to the sextant which are not adjustable and which can only be corrected by the sextant manufacturer.

Collimation error exists when the axis of the telescope is not exactly parallel to the plane of the sextant. This error causes the measured altitude to be greater than the real altitude.

Graduation error exists when the arc, micrometer or vernier, is incorrectly calibrated.

Shade error is caused by the faces of shade glasses not being ground parallel. This error is found by comparing the angle between two objects one time with shade up and the other with shade down.

Centering error is present when the index arm is not pivoted at the true center of curvature of the arc.

16

VERTICAL SEXTANT ANGLES

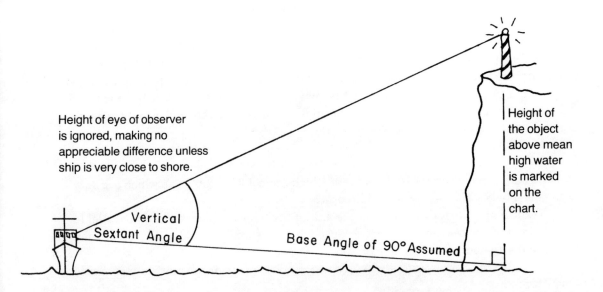

Height of eye of observer is ignored, making no appreciable difference unless ship is very close to shore.

Height of the object above mean high water is marked on the chart.

Vertical Sextant Angle

Base Angle of 90° Assumed

From the diagram it can be seen that: Distance off lighthouse = cotan of vertical angle × height of object. It is not usually necessary to make an allowance for the tidal difference from mean high water. Most sets of nautical tables contain a table on distance by vertical sextant angle. An extract from such a table is shown below.

Distance Off in Miles	Height of Object in Feet		
	200	220	240
2.4	0°47′	0°52′	0°57′
2.6	0°44′	0°48′	0°52′
2.8	0°40′	0°44′	0°48′
3.0	0°38′	0°41′	0°45′

Find the distance off a 210-foot point for a vertical sextant angle of 0°48′.
Interpolation is necessary halfway between 200 feet and 220 feet. That is, 0°49′.5 gives 2.4 miles and 0°46′ gives 2.6 miles for a 210-foot object. The given angle is 0°48′

which is about midway between the two. Therefore, distance off the point equals 2.5 miles.

After some practice with interpolation, these problems can be quickly done mentally by using simple proportion. If vertical sextant angle tables are not available, the following approximate formula can be used.

$$\text{Distance off (in miles)} = \frac{\text{half object's height (in feet)}}{\text{vertical sextant angle (in minutes)}}$$

It may be necessary to round a point or a beacon while keeping a certain distance from it to avoid rocks or shoals. The sextant angle necessary for such a distance off can be set on the sextant as a *danger angle*. If the angle increases beyond the set danger angle the vessel is setting too close inshore, and the helm is applied out until the danger angle is again reached. Thus, the point is rounded with safety if the danger angle is maintained.

The distance off computed from a vertical sextant angle will be the radius of a position circle with its center on the object concerned. Further information such as that obtained from a single bearing is necessary to fix the vessel's position.

Exercise:
Vertical Sextant Angles (Chart 13218)

1. Find the distance off a lighthouse 230 feet high if it subtends a vertical sextant angle of 0°45′.

2. What distance off the land would a vertical sextant angle of 0°47′ indicate if the height at that point is charted as 207 feet?

3. Find the distance off Southeast Pt. Lt., Block I., if it is subtending a vertical sextant angle of 0°39′.

4. What danger angle should be used to round a 235-foot lighthouse at a distance of 3 miles?

5. What danger angle would be necessary to round Southeast Pt. Lt., keeping 1½ cables outside the wreck marking the buoy off the point?

17

HORIZONTAL SEXTANT ANGLES

A single horizontal sextant angle gives only a position circle. The two objects concerned will subtend that same horizontal angle anywhere along the position circle. To find an observed position by using horizontal sextant angles, it is necessary to use two such position circles. The vessel will be at the intersection of these two circles.

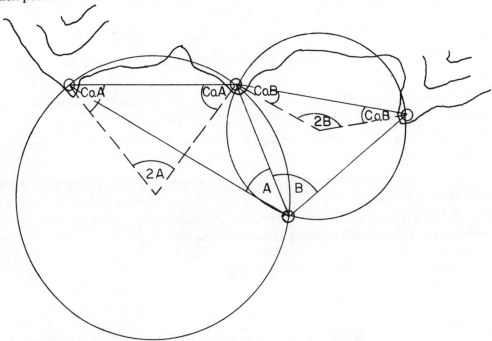

To construct the circles, a base line is drawn between the points concerned, and the complement of the horizontal angle is laid off from each end of the base line on the seaward side. (If the horizontal angle exceeds 90° lay off the excess of the 90° on the landward side of the base line.) The intersection of the lines from the base line will be the center of the position circle.

This method of position finding is based on the well-known geometric theorem that the angle that a chord subtends at the center of a circle will be twice the angle it subtends at the circumference. If the complement of the horizontal angle is laid off each end of the base line, then these two construction lines must cross at an angle twice the size of the horizontal angle. A circle drawn with this point as its center and the base line as a chord must, therefore, pass through all points where the chord would subtend this particular horizontal angle.

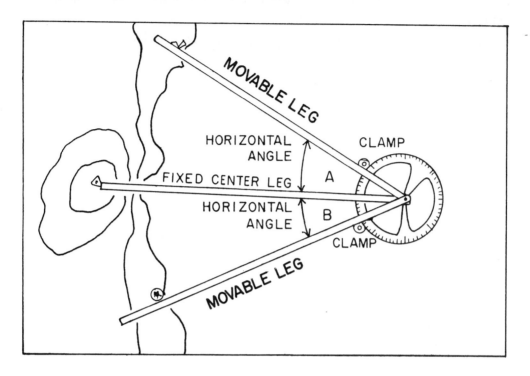

Use of the Three-Arm Protractor

The station pointer consists of a 360-degree protractor with a fixed center leg and two adjustable side legs. The horizontal angles are set on the instrument, and the legs are clamped in position. The instrument is then maneuvered on the chart until each leg lies on its appropriate landmark. The vessel's position can then be marked through the small hole in the center of the station pointer.

Horizontal sextant angles are not used a great deal for chartwork but are useful in checking a vessel's anchorage position. The two angles can be set up on separate sextants; any deviation from these horizontal sextant angles indicates movement of the vessel.

The compass error can also be checked by noting any differences between true bearings on the chart (from the position established by plotting horizontal sextant angles) and observed compass bearings of the same objects.

Exercise:
Horizontal Sextant Angles (Chart 13218)

1. Give the latitude and longitude of a vessel anchored with Warren Pt. 56° Quicksand Pt. 78° Gooseberry Neck Tower.

2. At what distance from the River Ledge Buoy is a vessel anchored with Bonnet Pt. 51° Beavertail Pt. 55° Brenton Reef Tower?

3. How far off the breakwater is a vessel with Southeast Pt. Lt. 48° Aeronautical Lt. 110° Conspicuous House at Clay Head?

4. Give the latitude and longitude of a vessel anchored with Gay Head Lt. 63° Menemsha Bight Lt. 115° Cape Higgon.

5. Give the position of a vessel anchored with Weepecket Main I. 78° Woods Hole Dome 54° Standpipe.

18

RISING AND DIPPING OF LIGHTS

The visibility of a lighted beacon, buoy, or lighthouse varies as to its height, the intensity of the light, and the height of eye (H. E.) of the observer.

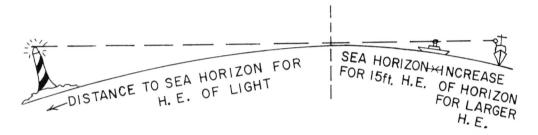

Range of Lights

The range of visibility of a "weak light" will be limited by its luminous intensity. However, the range of visibility of the rays emitted from a "strong light" will depend upon the height of that light and also the height of eye of the observer due to the curvature of the earth. (See diagram.)

All sets of nautical tables contain tables for the distance of the sea horizon for a given height of eye and also a table for the distance a strong light will be seen for a given height of eye and height of light. In computing the visibility of a strong light, it is always assumed that the light is sufficiently powerful to be seen at the computed range.

If no tables are available the following formula can be used:

$$\text{Range of visibility in nautical miles (approx.)} = 1.17 \left(\sqrt{\frac{\text{height of eye}}{\text{in feet}}} + \sqrt{\frac{\text{height of light}}{\text{in feet}}} \right)$$

Most lights have their range of visibility to the nearest mile indicated in their abbreviated characteristics listed on the chart itself. This range is often computed for a standard height of eye of 15 feet.

A vessel steaming toward the light from seaward may see the glow or the loom of the light pulsating from below the horizon. As the light is approached the light will suddenly appear. To check maximum range the light may be "bobbed" by alternately lowering and raising the height of eye to make the light disappear and then appear again.

The table for rising and dipping distance is computed for atmospheric conditions of normal refraction. Conditions of abnormal refraction, such as those created by warm air over cooler sea, can result in the normal rising distance being exceeded. Occasionally, lights may be seen to rise at two or three times their predicted range under extreme conditions of abnormal refraction.

The computed range of visibility of a given light for a given height of eye gives a position circle somewhere along which the vessel will lie. Additional information, such as a bearing, is required for a fix. The position circle can be used in a method similar to that for the transferred position line, as shown in the following diagram. It is usually obvious which of the two intersections in the diagram is the observed position.

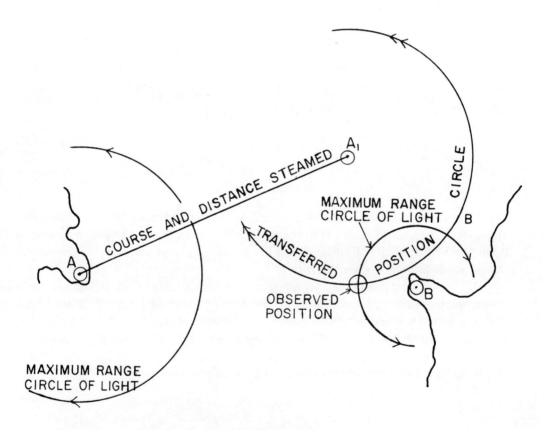

The Rule of Sixty

Head directly to the light at rising distance (distance in nautical miles). Alteration of course necessary in order to pass X in nautical miles abeam the light is approximately $(60/d) \times X$ degrees.

For example, rising distance d equals 15 nautical miles required to pass 5 nautical miles off the light; alteration of course necessary from light directly ahead equals (60/15) × 5 equals 20°.

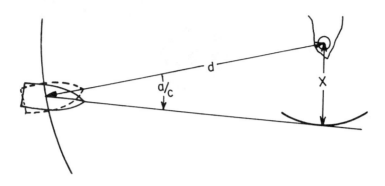

Exercise:
Rising and Dipping Distances (Chart 13009)

1. Give the latitude and longitude of a vessel with a height of eye of 25 feet if Cape Sable Lt. rises bearing 045° C, and the vessel is steering due east by compass using Deviation Card I.

2. Nantucket Shoals Lightship rose bearing 225° C to a vessel steering 306° C. Give the vessel's position if her height of eye is 32 feet, and she is using Deviation Card I.

3. Give the position of a vessel steering due west by compass if Highland Lt. rose bearing 250° C. Use Deviation Card II and a height of eye of 28 feet.

4. If Eastern Pt. (Cape Ann) Lt. dips bearing 328° C to a vessel with height of eye 30 feet, steering 165° C, how many miles should this vessel steam before Highland Lt. rises? Use Deviation Card I.

5. At 0400 Seal I. Lt. dipped, and the vessel steered 310° T at 10 knots. At 0600 Cape St. Mary Lt. rose. Find the vessel's position if the height of eye is 20 feet.

6. Matinicus Rock Lt. dipped to a vessel steering 056° T at 8 knots. One hour 15 minutes later Mt. Desert Rock Lt. rose. Find the vessel's position if the height of eye is 32 feet.

7. Nantucket Shoals Lightship dipped astern of a vessel which had a height of eye of 32 feet and which was steaming at 10 knots. Three hours later Sankaty Hd. Lt. rose. Give the vessel's position if she was steaming 316° C, using Deviation Card II.

8. Highland Lt. dipped at 0330 to a vessel steaming 342° C at 12 knots near Stellwagen Bank. One hour later Eastern Pt. (Cape Ann) Lt. rose. Give the vessel's position at 0430 if the height of eye was 20 feet. Use Deviation Card I.

9. A vessel is approaching Highland Lt. steering due west when the light rises directly ahead. What alteration of course is necessary to leave the light 5 nautical miles to port when abeam? Height of eye of observer is 13 feet.

19

LINES OF SOUNDINGS

If after fishing for some time you are unsure of your vessel's position, a good estimation can be made from soundings. These should be taken at regular intervals, approximately the steaming distance apart that the chart soundings are spaced. Mark these soundings on a straight edge graduated to the distance scale of the chart. The straight edge can then be angled on the chart to roughly correspond with the course steered, and can be moved around until the soundings appear to correspond with the depths marked on the chart. This method of position finding should not be relied upon entirely; as soon as land is neared and other means become available, the position should be checked.

On Chart 13009 the soundings are spaced about 3 miles apart. A 12-knot vessel would take soundings every 15 minutes. A stiff paper straightedge could then be marked with graduations from the latitude scale at 3-mile intervals and with the corresponding soundings. With the first sounding as a point of departure, the straightedge is angled on the chart at approximately the course steered. The final position is estimated when the soundings match up.

Exercise:
Lines of Soundings (Chart 13009)

1. A vessel in the vicinity of Lindenkohl Knoll proceeded on a westerly course recording soundings at half-hour intervals as follows: 99 fathoms, 117 fathoms, 103 fathoms, 97 fathoms, 104 fathoms, 106 fathoms, 110 fathoms, 93 fathoms. State the compass course made good and the position at the time of the last sounding if her steaming speed is estimated at 12 knots. Use Deviation Card I.

2. A vessel, with height of eye of 20 feet, steering 247° C at about 10 knots records the following soundings at half-hour intervals, starting at 0100: 5 fathoms, 10 fathoms, 20 fathoms, 33 fathoms, 29 fathoms, 37 fathoms, 32 fathoms. At what time should Nantucket Shoals Lightship Lt. be seen and at what compass bearing, if the vessel had been fishing near Little Georges? Use Deviation Card I.

3. A vessel proceeding magnetic northwest near Corsair Canyon crossed the 100-fathom line at 1100. The 50-fathom line was crossed at 1134, 1138, 1150, and 1207. The 40-fathom line was crossed at 1250. What is the vessel's estimated position at 1300? The vessel is steaming at about 14 knots.

4. A vessel with a draft of 12 feet leaves the Winter Fishing Ground, Georges Bank, steaming at about 11 knots in rough weather and steering 296° C, using Deviation Card I. The following soundings were recorded at half-hour intervals: 30 fathoms, 25 fathoms, 6 fathoms, 31 fathoms. Estimate the amount that the vessel is 20 fathoms, 33 fathoms, 29 fathoms, 37 fathoms, 32 fathoms. At what timbeing set to port of her course. Should she continue on this course?

Note that the probability of obtaining a good fix by this method varies directly with the irregularity of the soundings in the area. A flat bottom renders the line of soundings useless. Consider the degree of confidence associated with your answers in this exercise.

20

THE THREE-BEARING PROBLEM

The three-bearing problem is a means of determining the course made good by a vessel sailing under the influence of an unknown current.

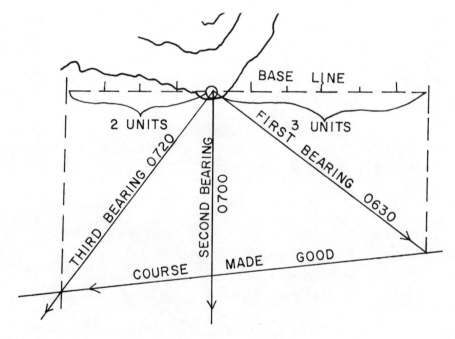

Three bearings are taken of a single object, and the time between each is noted. A base line is drawn through the object perpendicular to the center bearing. The base line is then marked on each side of the object in the same ratio as the time or log distance between the bearings. For example, if the run between the first and second bearings was 30 minutes and the run between the second and third bearings was 20 minutes the base line would be marked in a ratio of 3:2, as indicated in the diagram. Construction lines are then drawn parallel to the center bearing from the marks on the base line. The course made good will be a line joining the points where these construction lines intersect the first and last bearings.

It should be noted that this method determines the course made good only and is not necessarily the vessel's actual track through the water. The track will be parallel to the course made good but may be to port or starboard of the course made good as found. Further information, such as a sounding or radar distance from land, is required to fix the vessel's position at the time of one of the bearings, and then the course made good may be drawn through this point to give the vessel's track.

Exercise:
The Three-Bearing Problem (Chart 13218)

1. Brenton Reef Tower was bearing 002° T at 0500, 335° T at 0520, and 291° T at 0600. Estimate the true course that the vessel is making good.

2. Gay Head Lt. bore 088° T at 0700, 062° T at 0724, and 025° T at 0806. Estimate the compass course that the vessel is making good. Use Deviation Card I.

3. A vessel in latitude 41-20N observed Buzzards Tower at 1100 bearing 327° T. At 1120 the Tower was bearing 358° T and at 1150 it bore 038° T. Estimate the set and rate of the current if the vessel was steering 255° T at 7.2 knots.

4. The southeast point of Nomans Land bore 063° C at 0600, 039° C at 0618, and 005° C at 0654. If the vessel was steering 136° C, find the compass course she is making good. Use Deviation Card I.

THIRD GENERAL CHARTWORK EXERCISE
(CHART 13009)

Use Deviation Card I and assume the following: height of eye in the wheelhouse is 17 feet; steaming speed is 12 knots; trawling speed is 3½ knots.

1. Leaving Gloucester, give the compass course to steer from Eastern Pt. to a position 3.0 miles north of Boston Approach Lighted Whistle Buoy BD, assuming a current of 1 knot setting to the west.

2. At 0600, steering this course, you observe Highland Lt. four points on the starboard bow; at 0700 the light is abeam. What is the position of the 0700 running fix?

3. From this position you alter course to cross the traffic lanes at a right angle. What compass course is required to do this with no current or leeway?

4. At 0745 Highland Lt. has a compass bearing of 270° and subtends a vertical sextant angle of 00°34′.6. What is this position?

5. From this position you begin trawling along the 25-fathom curve in a generally magnetic south direction. At 1012, close aboard of Nauset Lighted Whistle Buoy 4, you haul back and steam on a steady compass course of 180°. You take compass bearings on Nauset Beach Lt. as follows:

Time:	1012	1030	1100
Compass bearing:	231°	270°	305°

What was the true course made good from 1012 to 1100?

6. At 1112 the 50-fathom curve is crossed with a Loran reading of 9960-Y-43975. What is the 1112 position? What was the set and drift (speed) of the current from 1012 to 1112?

7. From the 1112 position you steam for Great Round Shoal Entrance Lighted Whistle Buoy GRS. At 1148, with Chatham Lighted Whistle Buoy 6 abeam to starboard, you recommence trawling along the 25-fathom curve in a generally southeast direction. At 1400 you haul back and steam on a southerly course. Later, the following soundings were taken at 15-minute intervals, beginning at 1500: 10 fathoms, 4 fathoms, 3 fathoms, 5 fathoms, 13 fathoms. What is the 1600 estimated position?

8. At 1600 you recommence trawling on a compass course of 220°. At what time should you expect Sankaty Hd. Lt. to dip below the horizon?

9. At midnight, with a Loran reading of 9960-W-14000 in a depth of 20 fathoms, you haul back and set course for Nomans Land Lighted Whistle Buoy 2. What is this compass course with an average current of one knot setting northeast and a southerly wind giving 5° leeway? What is the estimated time of arrival at Nomans Buoy? With 30 miles between Nomans Buoy and your berth in New Bedford, to what passage speed should you slow the vessel so as to arrive at your berth at 0800?

21

THE SAILINGS

Thus far, most of the more practical aspects of chartwork have been discussed, and it is now important to introduce some of the basic theories of navigation. "Deep sea" navigation which utilizes observations of celestial bodies and information from electronic navigational aids will be explained in the second part of this text. However, four navigational sailings—plane, parallel, mid-latitude and Mercator—are included in this and the following chapters in order to introduce Part II: Marine Navigation. These chapters also serve as a connecting link between the two distinct fields of chartwork and navigation.

Moreover, for many fishermen and boat operators, these sailings provide substantial practical assistance in making full use of advanced electronic aids to navigation and fishing. Familiarity with these sailings will allow the correct determination of directions and distances without reference to charts. Familiarity with these sailings will allow the proper construction of large-scale charts of special-interest areas which might show, for example, corrected Loran position lines, hangs, fixed gear, clear tows, etc.

Plane Sailing

Plane sailing is the application of simple, plane trigonometry to simple navigational problems such as:

a. What is the course and distance to a point 40 miles north and 30 miles east of my present position? or

b. How far south and west of my present position is a point bearing 216.9°, distance 50 miles?

Such problems are solved by assuming that the shape formed by the meridian of longitude through the point of departure, the parallel of latitude through the point of arrival, and the rhumb line between these points is a plane (flat), right triangle.

(a)

In this triangle, *l* (the difference of latitude) represents the 40 miles north, and p (the departure) represents the 30 miles east in example (a).

With trigonometry, the course angle (C) can here be determined by the relationship

$$\tan C = \frac{p}{l}$$

which, in example (a) above, is

$$\tan C = \frac{30 \text{ mi.}}{40 \text{ mi.}} = 0.75$$

This means that, in example (a) above, the course angle (C) is the angle which has a tangent equal to 0.75. (C = arctan 0.75.) In this case, then, from trigonometry tables, C can be found to equal 36.9°.

Also, the distance (D) can here be determined by the relationship: D = l sec C = 40 miles (sec 36.9°). Thus, solving for the distance (D): D= l sec C = 40 miles × (sec 36.9°) = 40 miles × (1.25) = 50 miles.

Finally, in regard to the course angle, even more specific notation is called for. In this case, since l is North and p is East, the course angle is noted as follows.

$$C = N\ 036.9\ E$$

Thus, the *amount* of the course angle is determined by plane trigonometry, but the *direction* of the course angle is determined by inspection and the good sense of the navigator. This determination of course angle direction from course, or course from course angle, is a matter of convenience in using trigonometric tables and a matter of practicality in using calculated values. Examples of this procedure are shown below.

Course Angle	Quadrant	Calculation	Course
N 036.9 E	N E	000 + 036.9	036.9
S 036.9 E	S E	180 − 036.9	143.1
S 036.9 W	S W	180 + 036.9	216.9
N 036.9 W	N W	360 − 036.9	323.1

Course	Quadrant	Calculation	Course Angle
012.3	N E	012.3 − 000	N 012.3 E
123.4	S E	180 − 123.4	S 056.6 E
234.5	S W	234.5 − 180	S 054.5 W
345.6	N W	360 − 345.6	N 014.4 W

In example (b) below, a differently arranged plane (flat), right triangle might be drawn.

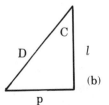

(b)

In this triangle, the course angle (C) is determined from the course (Cn) of 216.9 as is shown in example (b): C = S 036.9 W. The distance (D) is 50 miles.

With trigonometry, the distance south, called the difference of latitude (l), and the distance west, called the departure (p), can be determined using the following relationships.

$$l = \text{D} \cos \text{C} \qquad \text{and} \qquad p = \text{D} \sin \text{C}$$

Thus, in example (b), l = D cos 36.9 = 50 miles (0.80) = 40 miles, and p = D sin 36.9 = 50 miles (0.60) = 30 miles. Note that, since the course angle is S 036.9 W (in the southwest quadrant),

$$l = 40 \text{ miles S} \qquad \text{and} \qquad p = 30 \text{ miles W}$$

In actual practice, with correct determination of quadrant and correct notation of the direction of course angle, the plane sailing triangle is *not* altered to show actual direction in this way:

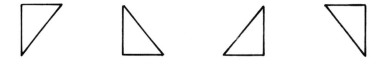

but is shown *only* in this configuration:

A final note on plane sailing:

Plane Sailing, by itself, will not provide longitude of the point of arrival but deals strictly with distance and course or course angle.

Solutions to more complicated problems involving all variables will follow.

Parallel Sailing

Parallel sailing establishes the relationship between difference of longitude (DLo) and departure (p), i.e., departure = difference of longitude × cosine of latitude.

As stated before in this book, the values of difference of longitude and departure between two given positions in the same latitude are equal at the equator, but as the poles are approached departure decreases to nil while difference of longitude remains the same. That is, departure varies from maximum at the equator to nil at the poles. Therefore, departure varies as to the cosine of the latitude. The proof follows.

Parallel Sailing Proof

To determine departure, or number of miles steamed along a given parallel of latitude for a given difference of longitude, first remember that the difference of longitude, or angle between the planes of two meridians, is the same in any latitude.

Thus, in the diagram, angle X = DLo
Then, the circular measure of X = $\dfrac{AB}{OA}$ or $\dfrac{CD}{EC}$

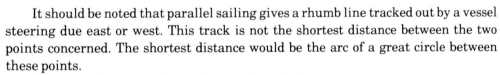

$$\frac{p}{OA} = \frac{DLo}{EC}$$

$$\frac{p}{DLo} = \frac{OA}{EC}$$

but, EC = EA (both radii of the sphere)

$$\frac{p}{DLo} = \frac{OA}{EA}$$

In triangle OAE
angle OAE = angle AEC (Alt. angles OA ∥ EC)

Cosine of angle OAE = $\dfrac{OA}{EA}$

Cosine of Lat. = $\dfrac{p}{DLo}$

It follows that secant of Lat. = $\dfrac{DLo}{p}$

$p = DLo \times \cos L$
and $DLo = p \times \sec L$

It should be noted that parallel sailing gives a rhumb line tracked out by a vessel steering due east or west. This track is not the shortest distance between the two points concerned. The shortest distance would be the arc of a great circle between these points.

Two examples of parallel sailing problems follow.

Example 1.

What distance in nautical miles is contained between the meridians of 169-47E and 173-00W in latitude 53-12N?

Note that the 180° meridian comes between these two longitudes. Therefore, each longitude should be subtracted from 180°, and the two differences added to give the total difference of longitude.

DLo = (180° − 169°47′) + (180° − 173°00′)
DLo = 10°13′ + 7° = 17°13′
p   = DLo × cos L
p   = 17°13′ × cos 53°12′ (1° = 60′)
p   = 1,033′ × cos 53°12′

No.	Log.
cos L = cos 53°12′	9.77744
DLo = 1,033	3.01410
p = 618.8	2.79154

Departure = 618.8 miles

Example 2.

At what speed would an observer in Lat. 01-12 rotate about the earth's axis?

The earth rotates through 360° of longitude in 1 day and, therefore, through 15° of longitude in 1 hour. The departure covered for 1 hour's rotation is required.

$p = DLo \times \cos L$

$p = 15 \times 60 \times \cos (01\text{-}12)$

$p = 900 \times \cos (01\text{-}12)$

No.	Log.
cos. 01-12	9.99990
900	2.95424
p = 899.8	2.95414

Speed of rotation = 899.8 knots.

Exercise:
Plane and Parallel Sailing

1. What is the course and distance to a point 108 miles north and 21 miles east of our present position?

2. What is the bearing and distance to a point 157 miles south and 54 miles east of this ship?

3. What is the course and distance *from* a vessel 57 miles south and 37 miles west of us *to* our position?

4. What is the course to and how long would it take, at a speed of 12 knots, to arrive at a position 18.4 miles north and 15.4 miles west of our present position?

5. Steaming on the following courses for the time spans and speeds (knots) shown, determine these differences of latitude and departures:

	Course	Speed	Time Span	l (N/S)	p (E/W)
a.	120	15	1200-1330		
b.	240	15	1330-1500		
c.	240	17	1500-1800		
d.	125	20	1800-2000		
e.	090	20	2000-2300		
f.	015	10	2300-0500		

6. For question 5 above, what is the total:
   a. difference of latitude (north or south)?
   b. departure (east or west)?

7. For question 5 above, what is the course resulting from the totals determined in 6 above between the start position and the 0500 position?

8. What is the departure corresponding to a difference of longitude of 003-42.0 (E or W) in latitude 37-56.0N?

9. What difference of longitude will a vessel cover steaming 820 miles due east in latitude 13-07.0S?

10. What is the arrival longitude of a ship which steams 714 miles due west from longitude 006-12.0E in latitude 57-18.0N?

11. In what latitude is a vessel which covers 008-40.0 difference of longitude in a distance of 420 miles?

12. At what rate is the Greenwich Observatory in latitude 51-28.5N being carried around the earth's axis?

13. How many miles does a vessel steam west from 005-12.0E to 008-04.0W in latitude 18-27.0S?

14. For question 5 above, what is the difference of longitude (E or W) corresponding to the total departure determined in 6 above? (See note below).

15. For question 5 above, what is the 0500 position if the 1200 position was 33-49.1N, 120-52.0W? (See note below.)

(For plane/parallel sailing, use the latitude of arrival to calculate the difference of longitude from the departure.)

22

THE TRAVERSE TABLES

The traverse tables establish the three sides of a plane right-angle triangle for all whole angles from 1 to 89° and all hypotenuses from 1 to 600 units. An example of the general layout of the table is shown below.

	333°	027°					**TABLE 3**						333°	027°
	207°	153°			Traverse	**27°**		Table					207°	153°
Dist.	D. Lat.	Dep.	Dist.	D. Lat.	Dep.	Dist.	D. Lat.	Dep.	Dist.	D. Lat.	Dep.	Dist.	D. Lat.	Dep.
301	268.2	136.7	361	321.7	163.9	421	375.1	191.1	481	428.6	218.4	541	482.0	245.6
02	269.1	137.1	62	322.5	164.3	22	376.0	191.6	82	429.5	218.8	42	482.9	246.1
03	270.0	137.6	63	323.4	164.8	23	376.9	192.0	83	430.4	219.3	43	483.8	246.5
04	270.9	138.0	64	324.3	165.3	24	377.8	192.5	84	431.2	219.7	44	484.7	247.0
05	271.8	138.5	65	325.2	165.7	25	378.7	192.9	85	432.1	220.2	45	485.6	247.4
06	272.6	138.9	66	326.1	166.2	26	379.6	193.4	86	433.0	220.6	46	486.5	247.9
07	273.5	139.4	67	327.0	166.6	27	380.5	193.9	87	433.9	221.1	47	487.4	248.3
08	274.4	139.8	68	327.9	167.1	28	381.4	194.3	88	434.8	221.5	48	488.3	248.8
09	275.3	140.3	69	328.8	167.5	29	382.2	194.8	89	435.7	222.0	49	489.2	249.2
10	276.2	140.7	70	329.7	168.0	30	383.1	195.2	90	436.6	222.5	50	490.1	249.7
Dist.	Dep.	D. Lat.	Dist.	Dep.	D. Lat.	Dist.	Dep.	D. Lat.	Dist.	Dep.	D. Lat.	Dist.	Dep.	D. Lat.

Dist.	D. Lat.	Dep.	**63°**	297°	063°
D Lo	Dep.			243°	117°
	m	D Lo			

Thus a plane right-angle triangle, with a course angle of 27° and a hypotenuse (distance) of 305 units, will have the side opposite the 27° angle equal to 138.5 units and the remaining adjacent side equal to 271.8 units.

So, the traverse tables can be used to provide rather quick and easy solutions to plane sailing problems. Take, for example, questions 5 and 6 in Exercise 18, for which the traverse tables are particularly suited.

	Course	Course Angle	Distance	Difference of latitude N	Difference of latitude S	Departure E	Departure W
a.	120	S 060 E	22.5	-	11.25	19.49	-
b.	240	S 060 W	22.5	-	11.25	-	19.49
c.	240	S 060 W	51.0	-	25.50	-	44.17
d.	125	S 055 E	40.0	-	22.94	32.77	-
e.	090	due E	60.0	-	-	60.00	-
f.	015	N 015 E	60.0	57.96	-	15.53	-
				57.96	70.94	127.79	63.66
					57.96	63.66	
		Totals (rounded off)			13.0 S	64.1 E	

Similarly, due to the relationship between difference of longitude and departure found in parallel sailing, the angle may be used as a latitude, and the values of departure and difference of longitude read off.

For example in latitude 27° N or S a difference of longitude of 305 minutes would give a departure value of 271.8 miles. This is because the cosine of the latitude equals departure divided by difference of longitude as proven. Therefore, the cosine relationship is provided by substituting difference of longitude for the hypotenuse side and departure for the adjacent side.

Therefore, parallel sailing problems can be solved by using the traverse tables, but take care to use the outer columns headed DLo and p—*not* the center column.

For angles or latitudes over 45°, the table is inverted and used in the same manner.

General sailing problems can easily be solved by substituting difference of latitude for the adjacent side, departure for the opposite side, and distance steamed for the hypotenuse side. The true course made good is substituted for the angle.

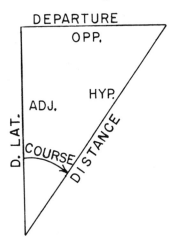

Note that difference of longitude cannot be used together with difference of latitude in a trigonometric relationship because their basic unit values differ.

If the angle, course steered or latitude, whichever the case may be, is not a whole degree, then the values of the sides of the triangle for the nearest degree below and above that angle are extracted and the required intermediate value is determined by interpolation. Or, in simpler words, the intermediate value is found by proportion.

For example, a departure of 276.2 corresponds to a difference of longitude of 310 in latitude 27°. For latitude 28° a difference of longitude of 310 gives a departure of 273.7.

If the departure for a difference of longitude of 310 in latitude 27°12′ is required then 12/60 of the difference between the departure values of 27° and 28° must be applied to the 27° value. That is, 12/60 or 1/5 of (276.2−273.7) is to be subtracted from 276.2. Therefore, as 276.2− (1/5 × 2.5) = 275.7, the required departure is 275.7 miles.

A detailed explanation of the traverse table is usually contained in the preamble to the tables.

With a good deal of practice, reasonably accurate interpolation can be carried out mentally and, thus, considerably reduce the calculating time.

As another example, the answer to question 7 in Exercise 18 can be determined by inspection of the traverse tables. Here, the course angle (C) at which the departure (p) equals 64.1 and the difference of latitude (l) equals 13.0 is determined, with interpolation, as S 078½ E. This yields a course (Cn) of 180 − 078½ = 101½. Also, the answers to questions 14 and 15 in Exercise 18 can be determined quickly by the traverse tables. First, calculate the arrival latitude:

$$33\text{-}49.1\text{N} − 00\text{-}13.0\text{S} = 33\text{-}36.1\text{N}$$

This arrival latitude is used, for plane/parallel sailing, to determine the difference of longitude (DLo) from the departure (p). Using the traverse tables, for L = 33, by interpolation, DLo = 76.4E; for L = 34, by interpolation, DLo = 77.3E; and so, by interpolation, for L = 33-36.1N (L = 33.6N), DLo = 76.9E = 001-16.9E.

Finally, the arrival longitude is calculated:

$$120\text{-}52.0\text{W} − 001\text{-}16.9\text{E} = 119\text{-}35.1\text{W}$$

Exercise:
Plane and Parallel Sailing by Traverse Table

1. What is the difference of latitude and the departure for a distance and course of:

	Distance	Course
a.	110 mi.	011
b.	166 mi.	161
c.	68 mi.	213
d.	24 mi.	320

2. What is the difference of longitude corresponding to a departure of 175.1 miles (E or W) in latitude 37-56.0N?

3. What distance will a vessel steam over a difference of longitude of 014-02.0E in latitude 13-07.0S?

4. From what east longitude has a vessel steamed 714 miles to arrive at longitude 015-49.6W in latitude 57-18.0N?

5. A sailing vessel beating through line squalls and a cold front logs the courses and speeds in the time spans as indicated below. Work the traverse from her 1800 star fix, at 37-57.4N, 068-33.1W, to her 2100 position.

Time Span	Course	Speed
a. 1800-1830	290	8.0 knots
b. 1830-1845	305	8.4 knots
c. 1845-1900	320	8.8 knots
d. 1900-1915	335	8.8 knots
e. 1915-1930	245	8.8 knots
f. 1930-1945	260	8.4 knots
g. 1945-2000	245	8.8 knots
h. 2000-2030	260	8.6 knots
i. 2030-2100	275	8.4 knots

23

MID-LATITUDE SAILING

Mid-latitude (or middle-latitude) sailing is a combination of plane sailing and parallel sailing. It is used to compute the change in latitude and longitude of a vessel steering a rhumb-line course, or, conversely, to find the rhumb-line course and distance between two known positions.

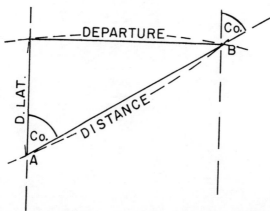

The spherical triangle formed by the sides of difference of latitude, departure, and distance can be treated as a plane triangle, without undue distortion, providing the distance involved is not too great.

Parallel sailing the latitude of A in the diagram will result in a departure larger than the mean value while sailing the latitude of B will give a departure smaller than the mean value. For this reason a mean of the latitudes is used when computing the departure:

$$Lm = \frac{\text{Lat. A} + \text{Lat. B}}{2}$$

Then, $\cos Lm \times DLo = p$

Mid-latitude sailing problems involve four quantities: course, distance, difference of latitude, and departure. If two of these quantities are known, then the other two are easily found by using plane trigonometry or the traverse tables.

For example, if the difference of latitude is known and the departure has been calculated by the parallel sailing method, utilizing the mean latitude, then the course and distance are calculated by:

$$\tan C = \frac{p}{l} \text{ and } D = l \sec C$$

Two worked mid-latitude sailing examples follow.

Example 1.

Calculate the course and distance from 43-27N, 022-12W to 46-18N, 018-08W.

43-27N	022-12W
46-18N	018-08W
02-51N	004-04E
×60	×60
l = 171N	DLo = 244E

$$Lm = 43\text{-}27 + \frac{02\text{-}51}{2} = 44\text{-}52.5N$$

	No.	Log.
$Lm = \cos 44\text{-}52.5$		9.85043
$DLo = 244$		2.38739
$p = 172.9$		2.23782
$l = 171$		2.23300
$\tan C$		0.00482
$C = \sec 45\text{-}19.1$		0.15294
171		2.23300
$D = 243.2$		2.38594

$$p = \cos Lm \times DLo$$
$$p = \cos 44\text{-}52.5 \times 244$$
$$p = 172.9 \text{ miles E}$$
$$\tan C = \frac{p}{l} = \frac{172.9}{171}$$
$$C = N\,45\text{-}19.1E$$
$$D = \sec C \times l$$
$$D = \sec\,45\text{-}19.1 \times 171$$

Distance = 243.2 miles

Traverse table check: p = 172.8, C = 45-20, D = 243.5 miles

Example 2.

Calculate the course and distance from 48-12S, 178-18E to 52-11S, 174-27W.

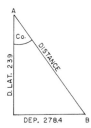

48-12S	178-18E	(through 180°)
52-11S	174-27W	
03-59S	352-45 from 360° =	
	007-15E	
×60	×60	
l = 239S	DLo = 435E	

$$Lm = 48\text{-}12S + \frac{03\text{-}59}{2} = 50\text{-}11.5S$$

	No.	Log.

$p = \cos Lm \times DLo$

$p = \cos 50\text{-}11.5 \times 435$

$p = 278.5E$

$\tan C = \dfrac{p}{l} = \dfrac{278.5}{239}$

$C = S\ 49\text{-}21.8E$, so $Cn = 130.6$

$D = \sec C \times l$

$D = \sec 49\text{-}21.8 \times 239$

Distance = 367 miles

	No.	Log.
$Lm = \cos 50\text{-}11.5$		9.80633
$DLo = 435$		2.63849
$p = 278.5E$		2.44482
$l = 239$		2.37840
$\tan C = \tan 49\text{-}21.8$		0.06642
$\sec C = \sec 49\text{-}21.8$		0.18625
$l = 239$		2.37840
$D = 367$		2.56465

Traverse table check: $p = 278.4$, $C = S\ 49\text{-}20E$, $D = 367$ miles.

Exercise:
Mid-Latitude Sailing

1. Find the course and distance between these positions:
   a. 23-18N, 014-12E and 26-42N, 017-07E
   b. 45-12N, 018-06W and 48-03N, 021-37W
   c. 17-06S, 045-12W and 21-14S, 047-06W
   d. 62-12N, 053-12W and 61-08N, 047-27W
   e. 01-08S, 178-12W and 01-09N, 176-47E

2. Determine the arrival position in these cases:

	Departure Position	Course	Distance
a.	13-12N, 057-18E	293½	286.4 miles
b.	61-12N, 084-16W	036.8	231 miles
c.	32-14S, 057-08E	342½	335.5 miles
d.	45-18N, 012-08W	271.1	322.7 miles
e.	02-00N, 179-00W	225	339.4 miles

24

MERCATOR SAILING

With mid-latitude sailing problems we found the course by means of the trigonometric ratio of the departure and difference of latitude of the plane course and distance triangle. These sides are expressed in units of nautical miles; for this reason it is necessary to convert difference of longitude into departure by the parallel sailing formula.

The Mercator sailing method uses the same two sides of the course-distance triangle, but they are expressed in units of longitude. The difference of latitude side is converted into minutes of longitude by the meridional parts table which is included in most sets of nautical tables. Thus, with the difference of latitude and the difference of longitude sides both expressed in minutes of longitude, the course angle is easily calculated. The distance is then found exactly as in the mid-latitude sailing method.

As previously explained, the Mercator method is preferable when the difference of latitude is appreciable.

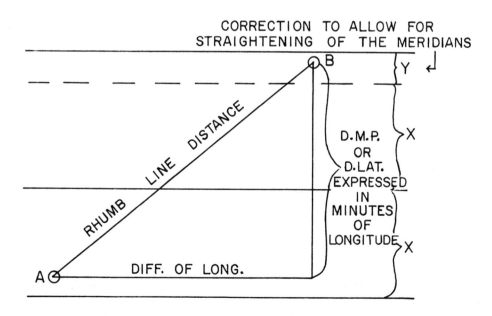

On a Mercator chart the latitude scale is increased by the secant of the latitude to maintain correct relative shape of masses.

Thus, scale of 1′ lat. = scale of 1′ long. × secant lat.

Because the latitude scale is variable, only small distances should be measured on the chart. Considerable discrepancy will occur when measuring large rhumb-line distances directly from the latitude scale.

The meridional parts for each of the two latitudes involved are extracted from the meridional parts table and subtracted from each other if latitudes have the same name, or added if the latitudes have opposite names. The resulting figure is the difference of meridional parts (m), or the difference of latitude accurately expressed in minutes of longitude.

Two worked examples of Mercator sailing problems follow. The use of a diagram is advised.

Example 1.

Find the course and distance from position A in 07-42N, 013-06W to position B in 24-18N, 006-02W.

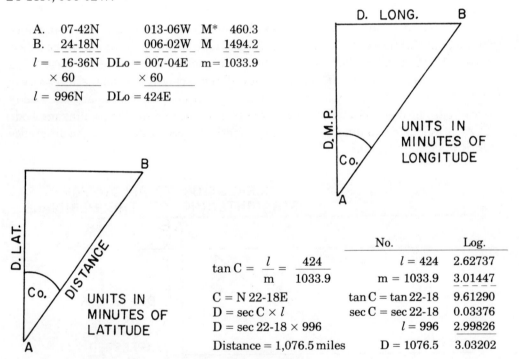

A. 07-42N   013-06W M* 460.3
B. 24-18N   006-02W M 1494.2
l = 16-36N DLo = 007-04E m= 1033.9
  × 60   × 60
l = 996N   DLo = 424E

D. LONG.   B

D.M.P. UNITS IN
MINUTES OF
Co.   LONGITUDE
A

B

D. LAT. DISTANCE

Co. UNITS IN
MINUTES OF
A   LATITUDE

	No.	Log.
l = 424	2.62737
m = 1033.9	3.01447
tan C = tan 22-18	9.61290
sec C = sec 22-18	0.03376
l = 996	2.99826
D = 1076.5	3.03202

$$\tan C = \frac{l}{m} = \frac{424}{1033.9}$$

C = N 22-18E
D = sec C × l
D = sec 22-18 × 996
Distance = 1,076.5 miles

Course from A to B is 022.3, and distance is 1,076.5 miles.

Example 2.

A ship steers a course angle of S 60°W from the equator changing her longitude by 900′. What is her arrival latitude and what distance will she have steamed?

*M is the value of meridional parts extracted from the tables.

	No.	Log.
$m = \cot C \times DLo$	$\cot 60°$	9.76144
$m = \cot 60° \times 900'$	$DLo = 900$	2.95424
$m = 519.6S$	$m = 519.6$	2.71568

EQUATOR   A

Meridional parts for equator are zero.
m in this case will be the meridional parts of arrival latitude.
M of 519.6 gives latitude 08-41.1S using the meridional parts table, so $l = 8 \times 60 + 41.1 = l = 521.1S$

	No.	Log.
$D = \sec C \times l$	$\sec C = \sec 60°$	0.30103
$D = \sec 60° \times 521.1$	$l = 521.1$	2.71692
Distance = 1,042.2 miles	$D = 1042.2$	3.01795

△ ABC IS IN UNITS OF LATITUDE
△ ADE IS IN UNITS OF LONGITUDE

Arrival latitude is 08-41.1S and distance steamed is 1,042.2 miles.

Exercise:
Mercator Sailing

1. Find the course and distance between these positions:
   a. 28-13N, 006-14E and 01-04S, 005-07W
   b. 03-17S, 053-12E and 08-14N, 072-17E
   c. 17-12N, 169-14W and 34-08N, 123-46W
   d. 42-08S, 169-14W and 64-14S, 173-08E
   e. 13-07N, 054-12E and 43-08N, 106-47E

2. A vessel left 05-12N, 007-18W and steered 321 for 1,500 miles. Find the arrival position.

3. A vessel left 16-08S, 042-17E and steered 171 for 2,200 miles. Find the arrival position.

4. Find the course and distance from 04-07N, 162-14E to 08-16S, 173-06W.

5. Determine the vertical distance (along the latitude scale) between the parallels indicated of these Mercator charts with these scales:

	Lower Parallel	Upper Parallel	Scale
Example:	40-20.0N	44-08.0N	1:500,000 at 43N
a.	40-40.0N	41-23.0N	1:80,000 at 41N
b.	41-02.5N	41-38.5N	1:80,000 at 41-27N
c.	34-35.0N	45-30.0N	1:1,200,000 at 40N
d.	09-55.0N	12-05.0N	1:294,500 at 11N
e.	01-05.0S	01-05.0N	1:294,500 at Q

Example worked:

Distance along the latitude scale = m (cos 43) (6,076) (12) (1/500,000) = (2940.9 −
2634.0) (0.73135) (6,076 feet/mile) (12 inches/foot) (1/500,000) = 32.73 in. Note
that this shows the height of Chart No. 13009.

25

PLOTTING SHEET CONSTRUCTION

As was suggested at the beginning of this section on the sailings, plotting sheets—particularly large-scale (small-area) plotting sheets—can be very useful to fishermen and boat operators.

Plotting sheets in various sizes at various scales can be purchased from chart vendors. However, the sizes, scales, and availability of these are all limited. The navigator familiar with the sailings can easily (and with confidence) construct plotting sheets of any size to any scale.

Two methods of plotting sheet construction will be explained here. The first—called a plane or small-area plotting sheet—provides a very close approximation to a Mercator projection. The second—called a Mercator plotting sheet—provides extreme fidelity to direction and distance.

Small-Area Plotting Sheet

The plane or small-area plotting sheet with selected latitude scale is constructed according to the steps explained below.

Step 1.

Choose a numerical scale (e.g., 1 inch = ½ mile) at the central parallel.* Also, choose the area to be covered (or the size of sheet to use.)

Step 2.

Through the center of the sheet draw a vertical line to represent the central meridian. Divide and mark this line into units of difference of latitude appropriate to scale.

---

*A natural scale may be chosen instead (e.g., 1:40,000 at 40N) requiring calculation of a numerical scale as follows.

length of one unit l on sheet = 1 unit l on earth x 6,076 $\times$ 12 $\times$ natural scale

½ minute l = 0.5 mile (6,076 feet/mile), 12 inches/foot/(1/40,000)

½ minute l = 0.91 inches

Step 3.

Through the center mark on the central meridian draw the central parallel as a horizontal line, perpendicular to the central meridian.

Step 4.

Through this intersection of central meridian and central parallel *lightly* draw a construction line having an angle with the central *parallel* equal to the middle latitude (chosen in Step 1.)

Step 5.

Divide and *lightly* mark the construction line into the same units of difference of latitude as in Step 2. (This can be done by swinging arcs from the marks on the central meridian to the construction line.)

Step 6.

From these marks on the construction line drop perpendiculars to the central parallel, thus dividing it and marking it into units of difference of longitude. These divisions will be equal in amount to, *but shorter in length than,* the chosen units of difference of latitude.

Step 7.

Fully label, at appropriate intervals, the latitude and longitude scales. Additional parallels and meridians may be drawn as a convenience to plotting. The construction line may be erased.

For small areas (at relatively large scale), small-area plotting sheets will yield no significant distortion of direction or distance. However, for larger areas (at relatively small scale), Mercator plotting sheets will provide better fidelity to direction and distance.

Mercator Plotting Sheet

To construct a Mercator plotting sheet the following steps should be undertaken.

Step 1.

Choose a numerical scale (e.g., 10 minutes DLo = 1 inch*).

Step 2.

Determine the lowest and highest latitude which will bound the area of interest and look up the meridional parts for these parallels. For example, 38-30N (M = 2492.1) to 41-30N (M = 2726.2).

---

*This choice may have to be adjusted after Step 3 or Step 5 to suit the dimensions of available sheets of paper, acetate, or Mylar.

Step 3.

Calculate the vertical length of the latitude scale as follows. Determine the difference of meridional parts (from Step 2). Divide this difference by the chosen number of units of DLo per inch (from Step 1). For example, with a scale of 10 minutes DLo per inch, to cover the band between 38-30N and 41-30N, the vertical length of the latitude scale would be $(2726.2 - 2492.1) \div 10 = 234.1 \div 10 = 23.41$ inches.

Step 4.

Determine which meridians will bound the area of interest and calculate the difference of longitude between them. For example, 069-30W to 072-30W yields DLo = 180 minutes.

Step 5.

Calculate the horizontal length of the longitude scale by dividing the full DLo (from Step 4) by the chosen number of units of DLo per inch (from Step 1). For example, with a scale of 10 minutes of DLo per inch, to cover the band between 069-30W and 072-30W, the horizontal length of the longitude scale would be $(072\text{-}30W - 069\text{-}30W) \div 10 = 180 \div 10 = 18.0$ inches.

Step 6.

Through the center of the sheet draw a horizontal line to represent the central parallel. From the center of this line divide and mark it into chosen units of DLo. In the example suggested, this line would be labeled 40N, and 181 marks at 0.1-inch intervals would represent each minute of longitude from 072-30W at the left end to 069-30W at the right end.

Step 7.

Through one of these marks (perhaps at 071W) draw a meridian as a vertical line, perpendicular to the central parallel. From the central parallel divide and mark this meridian into units of difference of latitude. In the example suggested, this would be done as follows.

Interval	Meridional Parts	m	Length
41-30 to 41-00	2726.2 to 2686.5	39.7	3.97 inches
41-00 to 40-30	2686.5 to 2647.0	39.5	3.95 inches
40-30 to 40-00	2647.0 to 2607.9	39.1	3.91 inches
40-00 to 39-30	2607.9 to 2569.0	38.9	3.89 inches
39-30 to 39-00	2569.0 to 2530.4	38.6	3.86 inches
39-00 to 38-30	2530.4 to 2492.1	38.3	3.83 inches

Step 8.

Evenly subdivide and mark each 30-minute interval into chosen units of difference of latitude. This can be done using parallel rules or navigator's triangles and the longitude scale as a guide.

Step 9.

Fully label, at appropriate intervals, the longitude and latitude scales. Additional meridians and parallels may be drawn as a convenience to plotting. In this example, a natural scale can be calculated as follows.

$$\text{Natural Scale} = \text{m from 40-30N to 39-30N} / 10 \text{ units DLo per inch} \times 60 \text{ miles}$$
$$\times\ 6{,}076 \text{ feet/mile} \times 12 \text{ inches/foot}$$
$$= 78.0 / 10 \times 60 \times 6{,}076 \times 12$$
$$\text{Natural Scale} = 1{:}560{,}862 \text{ at 40N}$$

ANSWERS TO EXERCISES FOR PART I

Chart Scales

Page 8

1. 8.23 miles
2. 1.55 inches
3. 1:266,130
4. 3.92 miles
5. 15.50 inches

6. 1:260,400
7. 1:508,355
8. 1:364,800
9. 3.87 miles
10. 28.35 inches

Position

Page 10

1. 273° T × 2.15 miles
2. 41-20.1N, 071-24.0W
3. 248½° T × 2.4 miles
4. 41-13.9N, 071-25.3W
5. 215° T × 6.0 miles

6. 40-59.5N, 071-49.3W
7. 298½° T × 3.8 miles
8. 41-13.8N, 071-45.4W
9. 143° T × 5.9 miles
10. 41-02.6N, 071-29.8W

Fixing Position

Page 15

1. 41-00.7N, 071-43.9W, 21 fathoms
2. 41-12.3N, 071-40.8W, 19½ fathoms
3. 40-54.4N, 072-15.0W
4. 40-54.7N, 071-44.5W
5. 41-04.0N, 072-02.4W, 8 fathoms

6. 41-14.8N, 071-41.8W
7. 20 fathoms and 3.3 miles
8. 40-57.4N, 071-43.4W
9. 40-52.5N, 072-00.3W
10. 41-08.8N, 072-07.7W

Chart Symbols

Page 18

1. (a) Wreck showing any portion of hull or superstructure above sounding datum (above mean low water in this case); wreck always partially submerged.
   (b) Wreck over which the depth is known (55 feet in this case).

(c) Sunken wreck which may be dangerous to surface navigation (less than 15 fathoms over wreck). (This wreck has less than 5 fathoms over it.)

2. (a) Black and white vertically striped fairway (midchannel)

lighted whistle buoy with the letters "MP" on it. The light is white, showing the characteristic of the morse code letter "A" (.–).

(b) Black, lighted bell buoy with the characters "1BI" on it. The light is white, flashing at 4-second intervals.

(c) Black, lighted gong buoy with the numeral "3" on it. The light is green, flashing at 4-second intervals.

(d) Red and black horizontally banded junction (obstruction) lighted horn buoy. The light is interrupted, quick-flashing white.

(e) Unlighted red nun buoy with the characters "2NS" on it.

3. THE U.S. NAVAL AIRCRAFT GARDINERS POINT TARGET. U. S. Government property prohibited to the public. Area is dangerous due to live undetonated explosives. Fishing, trawling, or anchoring within a 300-yard radius of the RUINS is dangerous due to possible recovery of aircraft practice bombs containing explosives.

4. (a) Group occulting WHITE (3), 15-second period. (5 s on, 2 s off, 2 s on, 2 s off, 2 s on, 2 s off.)

(b) Alternating between occulting WHITE and group-flashing RED (2), 15 second period. (White: 10 s on, 1.1 s off; Red: 0.3 s on, 2.2 s off, 0.3 s on, 1.1 s off.)

(c) Flashing WHITE, 5-second period.

5. FISH TRAP AREAS. Boundary lines of fish trap areas are shown by these dashed magenta lines. *Caution:* Submerged piling may exist in these areas.

6. (a) whS = White Sand
   (b) rky = Rocky

(c) hrd = Hard
(d) hrdS = Hard Sand
(e) Boulders

7. CURRENT DIAGRAM. Explanation: Directions and velocities of tidal currents at twenty-five stations are shown by arrows. The length of the arrow from the *center* of the circle represents the average velocity on a scale of one inch equals two knots. The figures at the arrowheads are the hours after the time of maximum flood (current) at Pollock Rip Channel, the daily predicted times of which are given in the National Ocean Survey, Tidal Current Tables, Atlantic Coast of North America. The velocities plotted should be increased by 20 percent (one-fifth) when the moon is *full or new* and decreased by 20 percent (one-fifth) when the moon is in *first or third quarter*. For effect of wind on tidal currents, see Tidal Current Tables, Atlantic Coast.

8. FISHERMEN MAY SUFFER DAMAGE TO THEIR NETS IN AREAS INDICATED BY GREEN TINT.

9. ∿∿∿∿ Submarine cable (power, telegraph, telephone, etc.). ------------ Submarine Cable Area ------------ cable area.

In view of the serious consequences resulting from damage to submarine cables and pipelines, vessel operators should take special care when anchoring, fishing, or engaging in underwater operations near areas where these cables or pipelines may exist or have been reported to exist.

Certain cables carry high voltage, while many pipelines carry natural gas under high pressure or petroleum products. Electrocution, fire, or explosion with injury, loss of life, or a serious pollution incident could occur if they are broached.

Vessels fouling a submarine cable or pipeline should attempt to clear without undue strain. Anchors or gear that cannot be cleared should be slipped, but no attempt should be made to cut a cable or pipeline.

In the event a submarine cable is caught in the fishing gear, notify the A. T. & T. Co. by telephone collect, giving position and details.

American Telephone and Telegraph Company
Bedminster, New Jersey 07921
201-234-6771

10. (a) Flashing WHITE, 5-second period.
    (b) Flashing WHITE, 5-second period.
    (c) Flashing WHITE, 10-second period.

True Course and Distance

1. 066° T, 24.7 miles
2. 103° T, 14.6 miles, 1¼ miles
3. 071-06.9W, 1 hour 51 minutes
4. 340° T, 1 hour 57 minutes
5. 057° T, 2153

6. 3 hours 04 minutes, 149° T
7. 312° T, 3 hours 34 minutes
8. 161½° T, 34.1 miles
9. 248° T, 25.5 miles
10. 060° T, 15.6 miles

Running Fix

1. 41-06.1N, 071-27.4W, 15 fathoms
2. 41-03.0N, 070-48.3W
3. 41-22.3N, 071-18.2W
4. 41-19.6N, 070-59.5W, 303° T
5. 41-25.0N, 070-47.9W

6. 41-10.4N, 070-55.9W
7. 41-07.4N, 071-22.5W
8. 41-20.4N, 071-32.6W
9. 41-25.0N, 071-17.3W
10. 41-23.9N, 070-50.8W

Variation and Magnetic Course

1. (a) 052° M
   (b) 085° M
   (c) 296° M
   (d) 333° M
   (e) 009° M
2. (a) 055° T
   (b) 159° T
   (c) 258° T
   (d) 010° T
   (e) 354° T

3. (a) 31° E
   (b) 29° W
   (c) 33 E
   (d) 9° W
   (e) 20° W
4. 300° M
5. 181° M

Deviation, Compass Course, and Compass Error

2. 4½° W, 2½° W, ¾° E, 3½° E, NIL
3. 5° W, ½° E, 3½° E, 2½° E, NIL

4. 5° E, NIL, 5½° W, 1½° W, 2½° E
5. 4½° E, NIL, 7° W, 1½° W, 5° E

6. (a) 156° M, 25° W, 153° C
   (b) 18° W, 225° M, 231° C
   (c) 274° T, 15° E, 259° C
   (d) 277° T, 29° W, 299° C
   (e) 033° T, 012° M, 4° W
   (f) 314° T, 332° M, 23° W
   (g) 22° E, 7° W, 15° E
   (h) 008° T, 4° W, 012° M
   (i) 205° M, 3° E, 202° C
   (j) 136° T, 4° E, 150° C

   (k) 43° E, 309° M, 315° C
   (l) 237° T, 5° W, 14° E
   (m) 151° T, 187° M, 11° E
   (n) 242° T, 23° W, 265° M
   (o) 21° E, 3° W, 18° E
   (p) 19° W, 018° M, 017° C
   (q) 319° T, 18° E, 301° C
   (r) 19° E, 30° E, 336° C
   (s) 350° M, NIL, 001° C
   (t) 000° T, 027° M, 41° E

Compass Courses and Bearings

1. Dev. 7° E, Var. 14° W, 40-58.5N, 071-40.6W
2. Dev. 1° E, Var. 13¾° W, 40-55.6N, 072-01.3W
3. Dev. 5½° E, Var. 13¼° W, 41-09.5N, 071-49.9W
4. Dev. 5½° W, distance 1 mile
5. 259° C
6. Dev. 1° W, distance 5 miles

7. 096° T, Dev. 3° W, Var. 13½° W, 112½ C
8. CE 15½° W, 138½° C, 15.3 miles; CE 21½° W, 201½° C
9. Dev. 6½° E, Var. 13½° W, 41-00.3N, 071-50.3W
10. Dev. 3½° E, Var. 14° W, 41-13.7N, 071-55.2W, 287° C

Doubling the Angle on the Bow

1. 4 miles
2. CE 9½° W, 41-20.2N, 071-07.1W
3. CE 22° W, 3½ miles, 3 miles

4. CE 21½° W, 41-12.1N, 071-27.7W
5. 2 miles

First General Chartwork Exercise

*1. (see footnote below)
2. 233½° C, 14 feet plus tide
3. 163½° C
4. 41-16.2N, 070-52.5W
5. 182½° C
6. 41-12.2N, 070-50.1W

7. 119½° C
8. 40-44.5N, 069-01.9W, 113½° T
9. 316½° C
10. 306½° C
11. 1552

*U.S. Charts of the 13000 series as follows: 13006, 009, 203-4, 218, 228-230, 233, 235-238, 241, 246, 260, 267, 270, 272, 278, 281, 286, 288, 292, 302, 312, 325. Canadian Charts: 4212-14, 4324, 4326, 4330. Look for: the edition date; whether chart is latest available edition (look in *Notices to Mariners*); whether chart is corrected to date. Allied publications: all *Notices to Mariners* since earliest chart or publication edition; East Coast *Tide Tables*; East Coast *Tidal Current Tables; Light List*, Vol. I; Canadian *Light List; Coast Pilot*, Vols. 1 and 2; Loran Tables; Pilot Charts.

Allowing for Wind and Current

1. CE 19° W, 156° C, 8.7 knots
2. CE 14½° W, 071° C, 8.3 knots
3. CE 24° W, 229° C, 6.8 knots
4. CE 14½° W, 301° C, 14 knots
5. CE 18° W, 151° C, 10.3 knots
6. CE 14° W, 107° C, 7.2 knots
7. CE 26° W, 184° C, 7.9 knots
8. CE 13½° W, 342½° C, 6 hours 58 minutes
9. CE 11° W, 339° C, 6 knots
10. CE 19½° W, 262½° C, 9.9 knots

Second General Chartwork Exercise

1. 155° C
2. 229° T × 2½ knots
3. 050° C, 1.1 miles
4. 41-25.8N, 071-02.6W
5. 064¼° C, 344° C, 1629

Tides

1. 6 hours 00 minutes, 7.9 feet
2. 6 hours 36 minutes, 4.4 feet
3. 0507, 0.1 foot; 1154, 4.0 feet
4. 6 hours 23 minutes, 3.8 feet
5. 0119, 4.3 feet; 0807, −0.1 foot
6. 1.4 feet
7. 2.4 feet
8. 0500
9. −0.3 foot
10. 0329/0827

Vertical Sextant Angles

1. 2.9 miles
2. 2.5 miles
3. 2.8 miles
4. 00-43.0
5. 03-45.0

Horizontal Sextant Angles

1. 41-27.3N, 071-05.3W
2. ½ mile
3. 6½ cables
4. 41-22.7N, 070-46.3W
5. 41-32.9N, 070-42.0W

Rising and Dipping Distances

1. 17.4 miles; 43-08.3N, 065-49.4W
2. 16.2 miles; 40-43.8N, 069-16.9W
3. 22.0 miles; 42-14.5N, 069-39.1W
4. 15.3 miles, 22.2 miles, 5.2 miles to go
5. 17.0 miles, 16.3 miles, 43-52.7N, 066-26.8W
6. 17.7 miles, 16.7 miles, 43-43.6N, 068-19.0W
7. 15.3 miles, 21.3 miles, 40-58.5N, 070-11.6W
8. 21.0 miles, 14.1 miles, 42-32.5N, 070-21.2W
9. change course to 285° T

Lines of Soundings

1. 268½° C, 42-13N, 068-30W   3. 1450, 277° C
2. 0652, 284° C   4. 15°, no

The Three-Bearing Problem

1. 066° T   3. 000° T, 1.2 knots
2. 178° C   4. 142° C

Third General Chartwork Exercise

1. 139½° C   6. 41-47.4N, 069-47.5W; 000° T,
2. 42-12.6N, 069-55.0W   2½ knots
3. 223° C   7. 41-12.8N, 069-38.0W
4. 42-03.6N, 070-00.0W   8. 1925
5. 135° T   9. 302° C, 0441, 9.1 knots

Plane and Parallel Sailing

1. 011, 110 miles   7. 101½
2. 161, 166 miles   8. 175.1 miles E or W
3. 033, 68 miles   9. 842.0 = 014-02.0 E
4. 320, 2 hours   10. DLo = 1321.6W = 022-01.6W
5. (a) 11.25S, 019.49E   start longitude = 006-12.0E
   (b) 11.25S, 019.49W   arrival longitude = 015-49.6W
   (c) 25.50S,044.17W   11. 36-07.8N or S
   (d) 22.94S, 032.77E   12. 704.11 knots
   (e) Nil, 060.00E   13. 755.1 miles
   (f) 57.96N, 015.53E   14. 64.1E (sec 33-36.1) = 76.9E =
6. (a) 13.0S   001-16.9E
   (b) 064.1E   15. 33-36.1N, 119-35.1W

Plane and Parallel Sailing
by Traverse Table

1. (a) 108 miles N, 21 miles E   (e) 0.93S, 1.99W
   (b) 157 miles S, 54 miles E   (f) 0.36S, 2.07W
   (c) 57 miles S, 37 miles W   (g) 1.99S, 0.93W
   (d) 18.4 miles N, 15.4 miles W   (h) 0.75S, 4.24W
2. 003-42.0 (E or W)   (i) 0.37N, 4.18W
3. 820 miles
4. 006-12.0E   sum 2.6N, 21.2W (rounded off)
5. (a) 1.37N, 3.76W l = 00-02.6N; DLo = 026.9W (from
   (b) 1.20N, 1.72W   the 38° Traverse Table);
   (c) 1.68N, 1.41W   latitude = 38-00.0N;
   (d) 1.99N, 0.93W   longitude = 069-00.0W

Mid-Latitude Sailing

1. (a) 037.9, 258.4 miles
   (b) 319.7, 224.1 miles
   (c) 203.5, 270.4 miles
   (d) 111.4, 175.8 miles
   (e) 294.5, 330.7 miles

2. (a) 15-06.2N, 052-47.2E
   (b) 64-17.0N, 079-13.8W
   (c) 26-54.0S, 055-12.0E
   (d) 45-24.2N, 019-47.0W
   (e) 02-00.0S, 177-00.0E

Mercator Sailing

1. (a) 200.5, 1,876.1 miles
   (b) 059.0, 1,341.3 miles
   (c) 067.6, 2,660.7 miles
   (d) 205.0, 1,462.5 miles
   (e) 056.7, 3,283.5 miles

2. 24-37.7N, 023-34.1W

3. 52-20.9S, 049-25.6E

4. 116.6, 1,661.4 miles

5. (a) 39.00 inches
   (b) 32.65 inches
   (c) 39.81 inches
   (d) 31.98 inches
   (e) 32.00 inches

Part II

MARINE NAVIGATION

H.O. Pub. No. 9, Vol. II, and No. 229, Vol. 3, are needed to complete the exercises in Part II. The necessary parts of the 1968 *Nautical Almanac* are in the appendix of this book. A table of increments from any year's *Nautical Almanac* may be used to supplement these. The use of Ageton's short method tables (*Manual of Celestial Navigation*, H.O. Pub. No. 211) is optional.

26

INTRODUCTION TO MARINE NAVIGATION

The text contained in Part II—Marine Navigation is intended to continue where Part I—Chartwork stops. The only presupposed knowledge is either a grounding in trigonometry and chartwork or satisfactory completion of the exercises in Part I on plane, parallel, mid-latitude, and Mercator sailing. A study of these sailing methods should help you make the transition between chartwork—plotting a ship's course in sight of land—and "deep sea" navigation—plotting a course out of sight of land. And, of course, many of the principles used in Part I can be applied to both celestial and electronic methods of navigation. (The principle of the transferred position line is one example.)

Celestial navigation is still the primary method of ocean navigation despite predictions of its replacement by electronic and satellite devices. However, professional navigators never cease to seek faster and better methods of sight reduction—the process of deriving from observations of a celestial body the information needed for establishing a line of position or series of possible positions of a vessel. It is doubtful that many of the operations at sea give the mariner the satisfaction that quickly and successfully reducing a number of star sights to a final observed position does, especially after navigating for a considerable time on dead reckoning in overcast conditions.

But, before you can attack such problems as sight reduction, you must first study the relevant associated theory. Thus, this text has been divided into two sections. The first section is confined to principles of navigation and the second to practical problems, including calculations and the use of necessary nautical tables. Both Part I and Part II have been pretested in classrooms and field work in the Department of Fisheries and Marine Technology at the University of Rhode Island over the last fifteen years.

27

THE SOLAR SYSTEM

The solar system consists of the Sun, its planets, and their individual satellites, all of which shine by means of the Sun's reflected light. The planets spin on their axes and move in elliptical orbits around the Sun with their orbital planes inclined at various angles. The farther away a planet is from the Sun, the longer it takes to complete one orbit. The relative positions of the planets, their distance from the Sun, and the approximate time for one complete orbit of the Sun are shown in the following diagram:

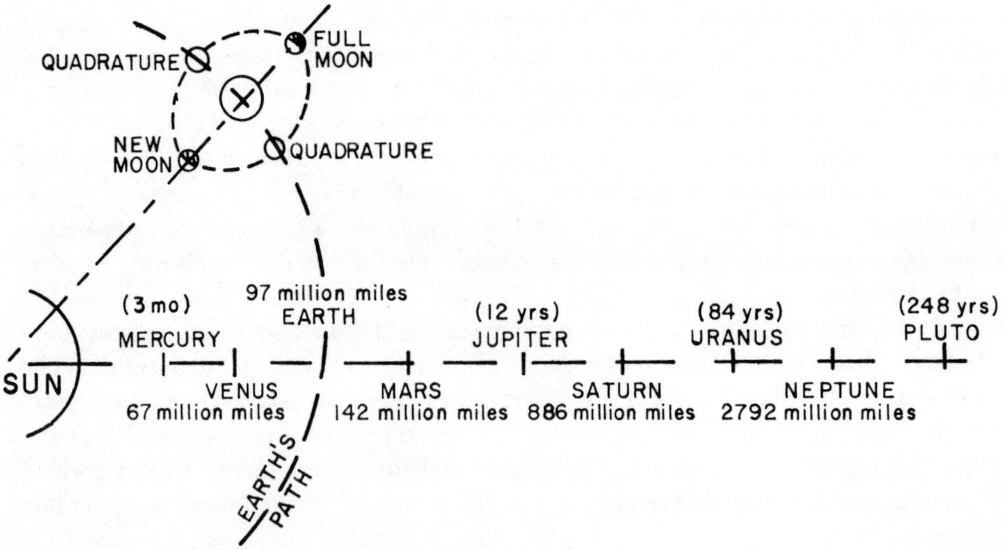

Bode's Law indicates the approximate relative distances of the planets from the Sun by adding four to each number in the series 3, 6, 12, 24, 48, 96, 192.

When the Earth and a given planet are in line on opposite sides of the Sun they are said to be in opposition. When they are in line on the same side of the Sun they are said to be in conjunction. If the Earth and a planet are 90° from each other they are said to be in a position of quadrature. Only the planets Venus, Mars, Jupiter, and Saturn are used for purposes of practical navigation.

The planets have a number of satellites, or moons, revolving around them while they themselves rotate on their axes as they orbit the Sun. The earth has only one moon, but other planets have a number of moons. For example, Jupiter has eight.

The planets Mercury and Venus, which are nearer to the Sun than the Earth, are termed inferior planets. All other planets are called superior planets.

Kepler's Laws

The Earth in its path about the Sun obeys three basic rules, known as Kepler's Laws. These rules, which apply to all planets, are described below.

Rule 1.

Every planet moves in an orbit which is an ellipse with the Sun at one of the points of foci. Similarly the track of a moon or satellite about its parent planet is also an ellipse with the planet at one of the points of foci. In the illustration, $d_1 + d_2$ is always constant, and the eccentricity of an ellipse is the distance of a point of foci from the center of the major axis.

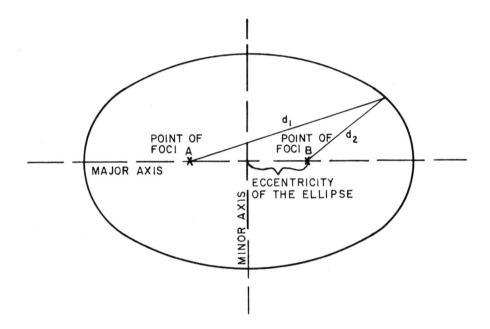

Rule 2.

A straight line joining the Sun to the center of a planet, i.e., the planet's radius vector, sweeps out equal areas in equal intervals of time.

Rule 3.

The square of the time taken for a planet to orbit the Sun is directly proportional to the cube of its distance from the Sun.

28

THE EARTH'S MOTION

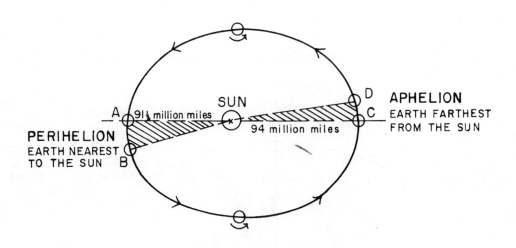

True Motion of the Earth

    The Earth rotates on its axis through 360° every 23 hours, 56 minutes, and 4 seconds as it revolves around the Sun in a counterclockwise direction once every 365.2422 days. That is, the Earth rotates once on its axis in about a day as it orbits the Sun in about 365.25 days. The Earth's path is an ellipse, and the Sun is at one of the points of foci of that ellipse. The Sun's diameter is about 100 times that of the Earth.

    It is easily seen from the diagram that in order for Kepler's Second Law to be obeyed the two shaded triangles must be equal in area, provided the time taken for the Earth to move from A to B is equal to the time taken to move from C to D. Clearly, however, AB is a greater distance than CD, and, in fact, the Earth's velocity must be faster at AB than CD.

    The Earth moves more quickly at perihelion (when it is closest to the Sun) than at aphelion (when it is farthest from the Sun).

    The Earth's equator is inclined at an angle of about 23½° to the orbital plane of the Earth.

Apparent Motion of the Sun, and the Seasons

On Earth we tend to imagine that we are the center of the solar system. Our true motion is taken up in the apparent motion of the Sun as illustrated below. But for navigational purposes we disregard distances in space and consider all heavenly bodies projected onto the inner surface of a huge sphere concentric with Earth. This sphere of infinite radius is referred to as the celestial sphere.

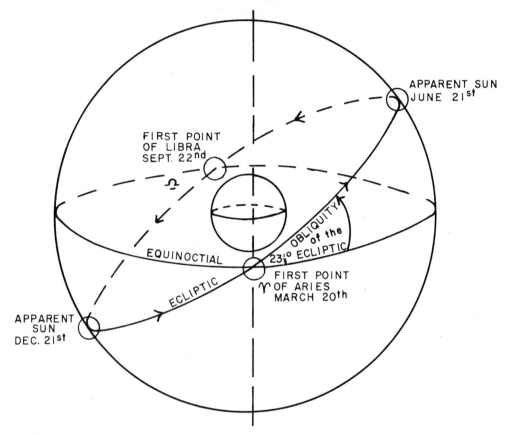

The path tracked out by the apparent Sun on the celestial sphere is called the ecliptic. The equator extended to the celestial sphere is termed the celestial equator, or equinoctial. The angle between the planes of the ecliptic and equinoctial is about 23½° and is referred to as the obliquity of the ecliptic.

This feature gives rise to the Earth's seasons. The northern hemisphere spring begins when the apparent Sun in its northerly path along the ecliptic crosses the equinoctial. This occurs on March 20, and is known as the vernal equinox and is also referred to as the first point of Aries, indicated by the sign ♈. Summer begins when the apparent Sun reaches its most northerly point on June 21 at the summer solstice. Summer ends when the apparent Sun, moving south, crosses the equinoctial on September 22 at the fall equinox. This point is also referred to as the first point of Libra, indicated by the sign ♎. The northern hemisphere winter begins when the apparent Sun attains its most southerly point on the ecliptic on December 21 at the winter solstice.

29

THE MOON'S MOTION

The plane of the Moon's orbit around Earth is inclined at an angle of about 5½° to the plane of the Earth's orbit about the Sun. The Moon is only about one-quarter million miles from Earth, and its diameter is approximately a quarter that of the Earth.

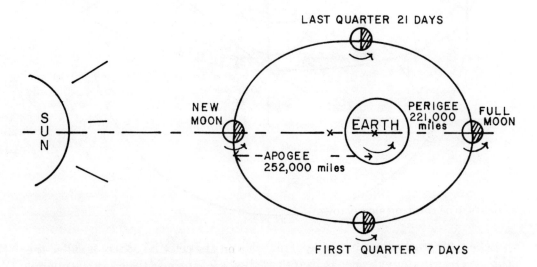

A lunation, the time interval between two successive new moons, takes about 29½ days. During this period, the Moon itself turns once on its axis and so always presents the same side to the Earth. Note that the Moon will complete a 360° circuit of Earth in about 27½ days, but that during this time the Earth has also moved in its path about the Sun, so that it will take about another two days for the Sun, Moon, and Earth to come back in line and the next new moon to occur.

30

THE STARS

The Principal Bright Stars

The multitude of stars in the heavens appears highly mysterious and complex to the student navigator. Stars have individual motion and many also move within a group just as Earth does within the solar group. However, because even the closest stars are such a great distance from Earth, this motion appears negligible, and the pattern of the heavens changes but little over hundreds of years. The nearest star is Proxima Centauri, which is 3½ light years from Earth. A light year is the distance that light travels in a year at the constant speed of light, which is about 186,000 miles per second. Therefore, one light year is about six million, million miles. Obviously, when dealing with such fantastic distances the light year is a far more expressive and easily handled unit of measure.

For purposes of navigation, these tremendous distances mean little. All stars are considered projected onto the inner surface of the celestial sphere and, therefore, of infinite and equal distance.

Observing the sky on a clear night, you will notice that the stars maintain the same configurations relative to each other, but the surface of the celestial sphere appears to be rotating slowly toward the west. Thus, stars to the west are approaching the horizon to eventually set, while stars to the east are climbing in the sky with other stars rising beneath them. This apparent motion is due to the Earth's rotating within the celestial sphere. Stars near the projected axis of the Earth will appear almost stationary. The star Polaris, commonly called the Pole Star, is very near the north celestial pole and remains almost fixed. All other stars will appear to describe small circles about the Pole Star.

As previously stated, the Earth turns through 360° in about 23 hours and 56 minutes. Therefore, the presentation of stars on the celestial sphere will appear to rotate once in the same time. Because time on Earth is kept with a 24-hour day, stars will rise and set about four minutes earlier each day. Thus, the overall configuration of the heavens will move to the west about four minutes of time or about one degree of arc at the same clock time on succeeding nights.

Individual stars are most easily recognized by their relative position within their group or constellation. Some of the more important stars used for navigation are shown in the following diagrams. They are shown in the position that they occupy in some easily recognized pattern with adjacent stars and constellations. The two principal constellations of the northern hemisphere are the Great Bear, or Plough, and Orion the Hunter. Most of the northern stars important to navigation can be recognized when related to these two well-known groups. Of the some 3,000 stars visible to the naked eye, only about 30 are used commonly by most navigators.

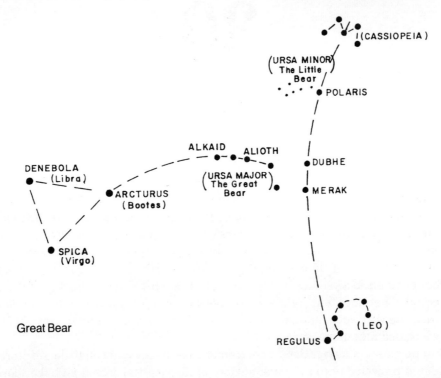

Great Bear

The principal bright stars near the Great Bear are easily recognized by following either the tail or the pointers of stars Dubhe and Mirfak as indicated in the diagram of the Great Bear. The constellations with which these bright stars are associated are shown in parentheses.

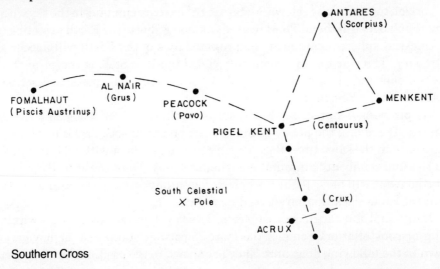

Southern Cross

The stars most often used for navigation near Orion are best located by tracing the three stars that make up Orion's Belt. Go one way to locate Aldebaran, and go the other way to locate Sirius, which is the brightest star in the heavens. The other bright stars then lie along a broad arc drawn between these two stars.

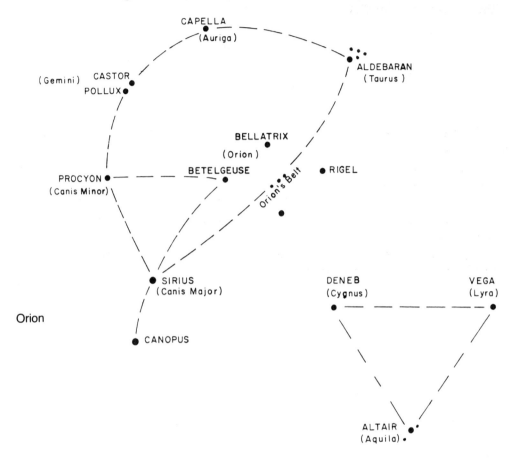

Altair, Vega, and Deneb

Other important stars of the northern hemisphere include Altair, Vega, and Deneb. These three stars are linked in an isosceles triangle pattern as shown in the diagram. Altair is easily recognized, having two small stars, one on each side of it, which line up to point toward Vega.

The principal constellation of the southern hemisphere is the well-known Southern Cross. The nearby bright stars are shown in the diagram of it.

Magnitude of the Stars

Stars vary a great deal in size and distance from Earth and their brightness is affected by these two factors. For example, the well-known bright star Capella is some 36 light years from Earth but, because its diameter is calculated to be as large as the Earth's orbital plane about the Sun, it is one of the brightest stars in the sky.

The system of grading stars according to their apparent brightness to the observer on earth was established about 800 B.C. by Hipparchus and Ptolemy. A star just visible to the naked eye is said to be of the sixth magnitude, and a star from which the Earth receives 100 times as much light as one of the sixth magnitude is said to be of the first magnitude. Thus,

$$\frac{S^6}{S^1} = 100$$

Therefore, $S^5 = 100$

Therefore, $S = \sqrt[5]{100}$

$S = 2.51$

Therefore, a rise of one magnitude of star indicates a 2.5 times increase in brightness.

The stars Sirius and Canopus are so bright that they require negative magnitudes. In fact, Sirius has a magnitude of -1.6 and Canopus, -0.9.

If we compare Sirius -1.6 with the star Regulus 1.3, we note that there are 2.9 intervening magnitudes. Therefore Sirius would appear $(2.51)^{2.9}$, or nearly 16 times, brighter than Regulus.

The magnitudes of selected stars are listed in the *Nautical Almanac*, a publication which will be discussed later in the text.

31

TIME

When discussing the true motion of the Earth we noted that, according to Kepler's Second Law, the Earth moves at varying speeds along its orbital path. When this motion is applied to the relative motion of the apparent Sun, its speed also must vary as it moves around the ecliptic.

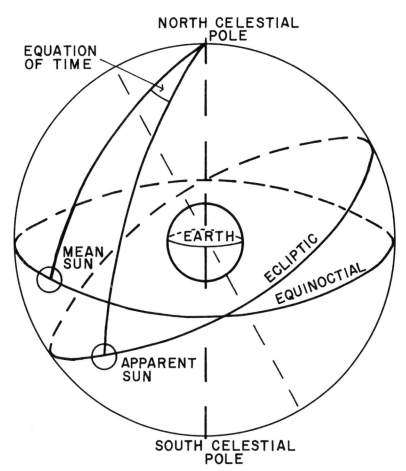

On Earth we keep solar time which uses a 24-hour day based on the movement of Earth around the Sun. Obviously the essense of time is a constant base, but since the apparent Sun does not provide this, we use a theoretical Sun. This mean, or astronomical mean, Sun is conceived to move along the equinoctial at a uniform rate and is the Sun on which our time is based.

We know that the apparent Sun will be moving faster at perihelion than at aphelion in order to sweep out equal areas of orbital plane in the same time. The mean Sun, however, moves at a constant speed. It is obvious, therefore, that at times the apparent Sun will be ahead of the mean Sun and at other times will be behind it.

The apparent Sun that we actually see and the mean Sun that we imagine are only in the same position at the times of perihelion and aphelion. In 1968 the mean and apparent suns coincided on April 15 and September 1.

The origin of our time system is Greenwich mean time (G.M.T.). The G.M.T. day begins when the mean Sun crosses the Greenwich *midnight* meridian and progresses one hour for each 15° of the mean Sun's westerly motion beyond this meridian. Greenwich noon occurs when the mean Sun reaches the Greenwich, or prime, meridian from which longitude is measured. However, we are only able to observe the apparent Sun and, therefore, require some link to establish the position of the mean Sun. This link is computed for each day and listed in the *Nautical Almanac* as the equation of time.

The Equation of Time

The equation of time is the excess of mean time over apparent time. The equation of time has a positive value when the mean Sun is ahead of the apparent Sun and a negative value when the mean Sun is behind the apparent Sun. When the positions of the mean and apparent Suns coincide, the value of the equation of time is zero.

Values for the equation of time are listed in the *Nautical Almanac* without signs because the sign conventions of the United States and the United Kingdom differ in respect to it.

The following diagrams are in the plane of the equinoctial with the north celestial pole at the center.

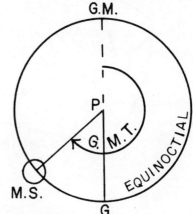

G.	Greenwich, or prime, meridian
G.M.	Greenwich midnight, or 180°, meridian
O.	observer's meridian
O.M.	observer's lower, or midnight, meridian
M.S.	mean Sun
A.S.	apparent Sun

Greenwich mean time (G.M.T.) is the angle at the celestial pole subtended by the Greenwich midnight meridian and the meridian passing through the

mean Sun, measured westward from
the Greenwich midnight meridian from
0 to 24 hours. Since 24 hours equals
360°, one hour equals 15°.

Greenwich apparent time (G.A.T.)
is the angle at the celestial pole subtended by the Greenwich midnight meridian and the meridian passing
through the apparent Sun, measured
westward from G.M. from 0 to 24 hours.

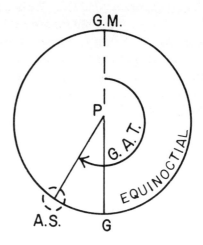

Equation of time (eq. of time), the
excess of mean over apparent time, is
positive when the mean Sun is ahead of
the apparent Sun. Thus,

G.A.T. $\pm$ eq. of time = G.M.T.

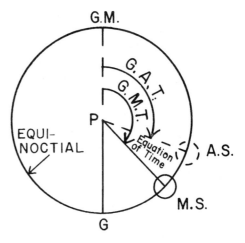

Local mean time (L.M.T.) is the
angle at the celestial pole subtended by
the observer's midnight meridian and
the meridian passing through the mean
Sun, measured westward from the observer's midnight meridian from 0 to 24
hours.

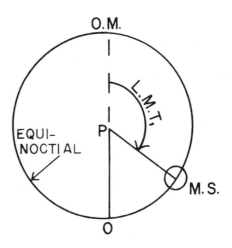

Local apparent time (L.A.T.) is the angle at the celestial pole subtended by the observer's midnight meridian and the meridian passing through the apparent Sun, measured westward from the observer's midnight meridian from 0 to 24 hours.

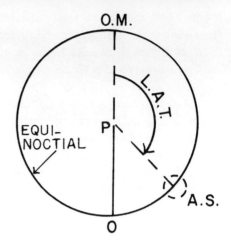

Equation of time, the excess of mean over apparent time, is *negative* when the mean Sun is behind the apparent Sun.

L.A.T. ± eq. of time = L.M.T.

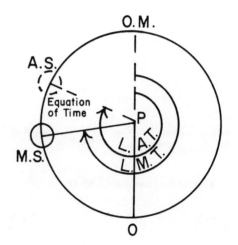

The Civil Calendar

The Mean Solar Day

The mean solar day is the time taken for two successive transits of a stationary observer's meridian with the mean Sun. This results in a constant 24-hour day which is the mean of all the apparent solar days of the year.

The Sidereal Day

The sidereal day is the time taken for two successive transits of a stationary observer's meridian with Aries or any distant star. It is the time taken for a given meridian to turn through 360° and is a constant 23 hours 56 minutes 4 seconds.

The Lunar Day

The lunar day is the time taken for two successive transits of a stationary observer's meridian with the Moon. While the Earth rotates once, the Moon moves about 12° along its orbital path. Taking this motion into consideration, we find a lunar day of about 24 hours and 50 minutes.

The Calendar

Our calendar system was devised by Pope Gregory in about 1600. The Earth takes exactly 365.2422 days to orbit the Sun. This necessitates a calendar year of 365 days with an extra day added to give a 366-day leap year every fourth year when the last two figures of the year are divisible by four. For example, 1972 was a leap year. This brings the resultant year to 365¼ days. To further refine this, there is no leap year at the turn of a century unless the first two figures are divisible by four. For example, the year 1900 was not a leap year, but the year 2000 will be.

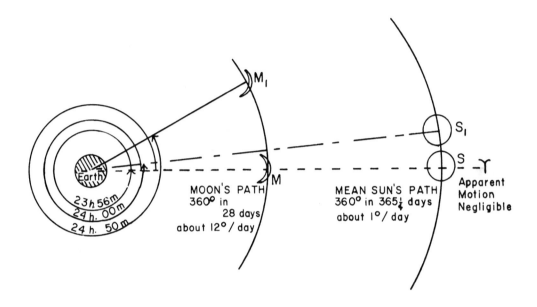

Longitude and Time

The following diagrams in the plane of the equinoctial illustrate the longitude relationship between local and Greenwich time.

G.M.T. + long. east = L.M.T.

When converting longitude to time remember:

15° = 1 hour. Therefore, 15′ = 1 minute.
1° = 4 minutes. Therefore, 1′ = 4 seconds.

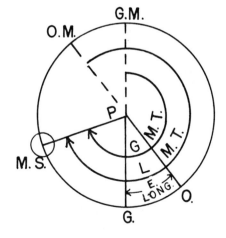

G.M.T. − long. west = L.M.T.

    An easily remembered rule which establishes the longitude relationship of Greenwich to local time is:

Longitude west Greenwich time best;
Longitude east Greenwich time least.

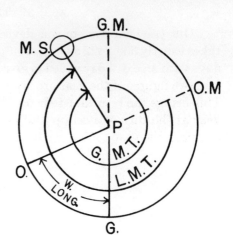

G.A.T. − long. west = L.A.T.

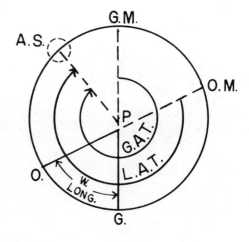

L.A.T. + eq. of time + long. west = G.M.T.
G.A.T. + eq. of time − long. west = L.M.T.

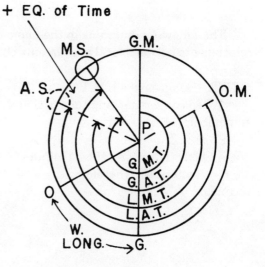

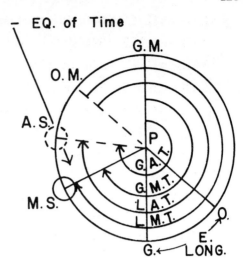

L.A.T. − eq. of time − long. east =
G.M.T.
G.A.T. − eq. of time + long. east =
L.M.T.

Zone Time

In order to keep the Sun somewhere near the meridian at local noon time, it is necessary to lag the time of noon behind 1200 at Greenwich in westerly longitudes and advance the time of noon ahead of 1200 at Greenwich in easterly longitudes.

Because 15° of longitude represent one hour of time, all longitudes within 7½° east and west come within the Greenwich zone. Between 7½° and 22½° west longitude, a zone time of *plus* 1 hour is in effect, so that 1 hour is to be added to local time to obtain Greenwich time. Conversely, between the longitudes of 7½° and 22½° east, a zone time of *minus* 1 hour exists, so that 1 hour is to be subtracted from local time to obtain Greenwich time.

For each successive 15° west, the zone time is an additional hour behind Greenwich time and for each successive 15° east the zone time is 1 additional hour ahead of Greenwich time. Clearly then, a vessel approaching the 180° meridian going west would be keeping time 12 hours behind Greenwich time, while a vessel approaching the same meridian going east would be keeping time 12 hours ahead of Greenwich. To account for the 24-hour time difference, the international date line has been estabished in the vicinity of the 180° meridian, and the vessel's calendar gains a day going eastward and loses a day going westward.

Some countries are vast enough to contain many time zones; for instance, Russia has 11. India simplifies matters by keeping a mean zone time of minus 5½ hours.

Exercise:
Time

Answers to all exercises in Part II are on pages 167 to 168.

A diagram in the plane of the equinoctial should accompany each calculation. Remember that (1) the equation of time is the excess of mean time over apparent time and (2) if longitude west, Greenwich time is best.

1. Given G.M.T. 0530, state the L.M.T. of an observer in longitude 045-00W.

2. Given L.M.T. 1624, state the G.M.T. of an observer in longitude 073-00E.

3. Given G.A.T. 0220 and eq. of time −3m12s, state G.M.T.

4. Given L.M.T. 2317 and eq. of time + 6m43s, state L.A.T.

5. Given G.A.T. 11h27m24s and longitude of observer 023-44E, find L.A.T.

6. If L.A.T. is 13h02m20s and eq. of time is −7m49s, find L.M.T.

7. An observer in longitude 078-12W has L.A.T. 1622. If the eq. of time is +3m18s find the G.M.T.

8. If the G.M.T. of an observer in longitude 023-12E is 0729 and the eq. of time is −6m21s, find the L.A.T.

9. If an observer in longitude 069-18E has an L.A.T. of 0214 on July 20, calculate the G.M.T. if the equation of time is +3m12s.

10. An observer in longitude 123-12W has G.A.T. 0523 on December 22. Calculate the L.M.T. of the observer if the eq. of time is −3m40s.

32

CELESTIAL SPHERE

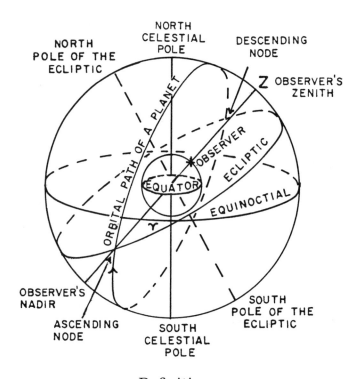

Definitions

Observer's Zenith and Nadir

The point where a straight line drawn from the center of the Earth through the observer's position on Earth meets the celestial sphere is called the observer's zenith. The point on the celestial sphere directly opposite the observer's zenith is called the observer's nadir. The great circle on the celestial sphere, whose plane is perpendicular to the line joining the observer's zenith and nadir, is known as the observer's celestial, or rational, horizon. The importance of the rational horizon will become evident in studying the section on sextant altitude correction.

Geographical Position

This is the point on the earth's surface cut by a straight line joining a particular body to the center of the earth. The position on Earth directly beneath the Sun is known as a subsolar point and the position on Earth directly beneath a star is termed a substellar point.

Nodes

When the path of a planet is tracked out on the celestial sphere it will cut the ecliptic in two places. The point of intersection of the planet's orbital path, going from south to north, is the ascending node, while the point of intersection, going from north to south, is the descending node.

Celestial Poles

The points where the earth's axis, when projected, cuts the celestial sphere are known as the north and south celestial poles. Semigreat circles which pass through the celestial poles and correspond with the terrestrial meridians are called celestial meridians.

Role of the *Nautical Almanac*

In order to calculate a position from observations of celestial bodies, it is first necessary to know the exact position of those bodies on the celestial sphere at the instant required.

The *Nautical Almanac* tabulates the precomputed positions of the Moon, Sun, planets, and principal stars on the celestial sphere for each hour G.M.T. of the year. The *Almanac* also contains a table of increments so that the position of any of the bodies may be obtained for any particular second of the year.

Certain corrections and simple calculations reduce the angular distance of a body above the observer's horizon, as obtained by sextant observation, to a position circle on the celestial sphere. This celestial position circle is centered on the body observed; the observer's earth location, when projected onto the celestial sphere, will be somewhere along this circle. The intersection of two such celestial position circles will provide the projected position of the observer on the celestial sphere, i.e., the observer's zenith.

The latitude of a body on the celestial sphere, or angular distance north or south of the equinoctial, is known as the declination of that body. Greenwich hour angle (G.H.A.) is used instead of longitude to position a body on the celestial sphere. The G.H.A. is the angular distance of a body west of the Greenwich or prime meridian.

The *Nautical Almanac* provides the declination and G.H.A. for all the heavenly bodies normally used for navigational purposes for each hour of the year. Because the motion of the stars relative to each other appears negligible to us on Earth, it is only necessary to catalog the G.H.A. of one star for each hour. The star used is Aries; other selected stars are referred to Aries by their sidereal hour angle (S.H.A.). The S.H.A. of a star is its angular distance west of Aries. The S.H.A. and declination of the stars are listed on every other page of the *Almanac*, which means, in fact, at 6-day intervals. Very little change will be seen in the S.H.A. or declination of any star from week to week.

Hour Angles

The following diagrams are in the plane of the equinoctial with the north celestial pole at the center.

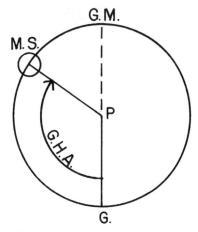

G.   Greenwich, or prime, meridian
G.M. Greenwich lower, or midnight, meridian
O.   observer's meridian
O.M. observer's lower meridian
M.S. mean sun
  *   star
  ♈   Aries

Greenwich hour angle (G.H.A.) of a body is the angle at the celestial pole subtended by the Greenwich meridian and the meridian which passes through the body concerned, measured westward from Greenwich from 0° to 360°. Note that

G.H.A. of mean Sun ± 12 hours = G.M.T.

Local hour angle (L.H.A.) of a body is the angle at the celestial pole subtended by the observer's meridian and the meridian which passes through the body, measured westward from observer from 0° to 360°.

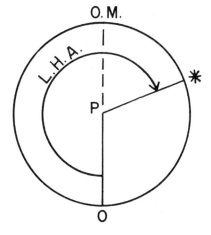

Greenwich hour angle of Aries (G.H.A.♈) is the angle at the celestial pole between the Greenwich meridian and the meridian which passes through Aries, measured westward from Greenwich from 0° to 360°.

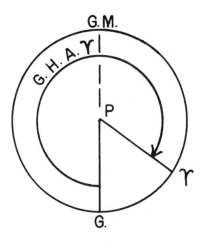

Sidereal hour angle of a star (S.H.A.*) is the angle at the celestial pole between the meridian which passes through Aries and the meridian which passes through the star, measured westward from Aries from 0° to 360°.

Right ascension of a star is the angle at the celestial pole between Aries and the star, measured eastward from Aries from 0 to 24 hours.

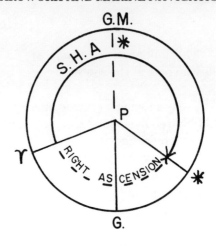

Greenwich hour angle of a star (G.H.A.*) is the angle at the celestial pole between the Greenwich meridian and the meridian which passes through the star, measured westward from Greenwich from 0° to 360°.

G.H.A.* = G.H.A.♈ + S.H.A.*

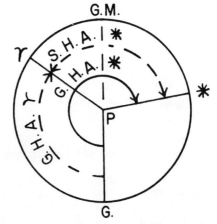

Locating a Body on the Celestial Sphere

The position of a body at any instant can be found by extracting its declination and G.H.A. for that particular moment of time from the *Nautical Almanac*. The above diagram illustrates how this system fixes a certain body X on the celestial sphere. Clearly the G.H.A. is the angle at the celestial pole subtended by the Greenwich meridian and the meridian which passes through the body, while declination is the angle at the center of the earth subtended by the equinoctial and the body.

A great circle on the celestial sphere which passes through the observer's zenith and nadir is known as a vertical circle. In particular, the vertical circle that passes through the east and west points of the observer's rational horizon is known as the prime vertical. The corrected true altitude of a body above the observer's rational horizon is the angular distance between the rational horizon and the body measured along the vertical circle through the body. The arc of that same vertical circle contained between Z and X in the diagram is known as the zenith distance of the body; clearly the sum of the true altitude and zenith distance of a body is 90°.

A body may also be positioned on the celestial sphere by its true bearing, or azimuth, from the observer's zenith plus its zenith distance. From the diagram it can

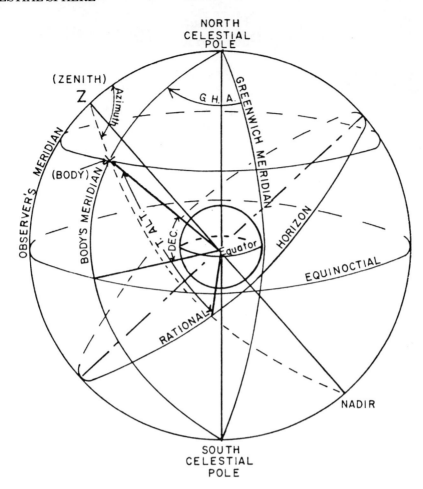

be seen that the azimuth of a body is defined as the angle at the observer's zenith contained between the observer's true meridian and the vertical circle which passes through the body. Obviously, if the exact position of a body can be established from the *Nautical Almanac*, then the position of the observer's zenith can be found by laying back the azimuth and zenith distance from the body.

Note that when a body bears due north or south from the observer, the observer's meridian becomes a vertical circle.

Also, note that throughout this text, the navigational triangle is labeled PZX, pzx to identify, respectively, the observer's elevated pole, the celestial body, the observer's zenith, the zenith distance of the body, the polar distance of the body, and the colatitude of the observer. Notation of these parts of the navigational triangle in ordinary American practice is as follows.

Interior angle at P = meridian angle (t)
Interior angle at Z = azimuth angle (Z)
Interior angle at X = parallactic angle (X)
ZX is p (side opposite P) = zenith distance (z)
PX is z (side opposite Z) = polar distance (p)
PZ is x (side opposite X) = colatitude (co-L)

Exercise:
Hour Angles

1. If the G.H.A. of star Sirius was 195° 27′, what would be the L.H.A. of that star to an observer in 057-13W?

2. State the G.H.A. of star Procyon if its L.H.A. was 284° 18′ to an observer in 113-18W.

3. What is the L.H.A. of star Arcturus if its G.H.A. is 12° 57′ and the observer is in 018-22E longitude?

4. Find the G.H.A. of the Sun if its L.H.A. was 36° 42′ to an observer in 057-38E.

5. If the G.H.A. of star Canopus was 342° 18′ and its L.H.A. was 297° 42′, what is the observer's longitude?

6. If the L.H.A. of the Sun is 357° 22′ and its G.H.A. 18° 16′, what is the observer's longitude?

7. What is the right ascension of star Capella if its S.H.A. is 127° 15′?

8. If the G.H.A. of Aries is 117° 52′ and the S.H.A. of the star Spica 206° 04′, what is the G.H.A. of Spica?

9. What is the L.H.A. of star Vega to an observer in longitude 042-18W when G.H.A. of Aries is 217° 08′ and S.H.A. of Vega is 87° 42′?

10. Find the S.H.A. of star Rigel if its L.H.A. was 182° 15′ to an observer in 169-18E when G.H.A. of Aries was 342° 17′.

33

INSTRUMENTS AND SEXTANT ANGLES

The Chronometer

It is a relatively easy procedure to determine latitude by observation of the Sun when it crosses the observer's meridian or by determining the sextant altitude of the Pole Star. Both of these methods will be examined later in the text. But it has only been in the last 200 years that sufficiently accurate and durable time pieces have been available to facilitate the calculation of longitude at sea.

And longitude determination is really a matter of accurate timekeeping. For example, an observer had the Sun overhead at noon in London, and then sailed west for a number of days with one clock set on London time. When an observation of the Sun as it crossed the observer's meridian indicated that there was exactly one hour's difference between the ship's time and London time, he had altered his position 15°.

In recognition of the importance of accurate timekeeping, a Board of Longitude was instituted in England in 1714 with a prize of £20,000 offered for solving the longitude problem. John Harrison, a Lincolnshire carpenter, devoted his entire lifetime to producing a chronometer to meet the board's requirements. In 1761, when Harrison was 68, his fourth version of the chronometer easily met all the accuracies demanded by the Board. On a voyage from England to Jamaica on the ship *Deptford*, the chronometer was only 5 seconds in error after a 2-month time span. This wonderful achievement by an uneducated carpenter confounded most scientists of the day, but was marred by the fact that the prize money was not awarded until Harrison was 80 years old. All of Harrison's original chronometers are still in good working order and can be seen at Britain's National Maritime Museum.

Today's chronometers are little advanced from Harrison's, but radio time checks allow constant daily checks on their accuracy. If the daily rate of time loss or gain is constant, then the accumulated error of the chronometer can be reliably computed by multiplying the daily rate by the number of days since the last radio time check was obtained. Chronometers are slung in gimbals and placed in well-padded boxes to protect them against vibration, temperature changes, and dampness. Temperature change is compensated for in the balance wheel of the chronometer. It is good practice to wind a chronometer at the same time each day in order to use the same part of the spring and also help maintain a steady "daily rate."

The chronometer is set on G.M.T., while the ship's clock is altered to coincide with zone time or some local time determined by the meridian the ship is on at noon. The importance of the accuracy of the chronometer can be realized when making the time-to-longitude comparison. Twenty-four hours of time represent 360° of longitude; thus, one hour of time represents 15° of longitude and one minute of time represents 15 minutes of longitude. Therefore, a 4-second error in chronometer time results in a 1-minute error in longitude.

Sextant Altitude Correction

In order to calculate the observer's position, the sextant altitude of a body above the visible horizon at sea must have certain corrections applied to it in order for it to give the altitude of the body above the observer's rational horizon.

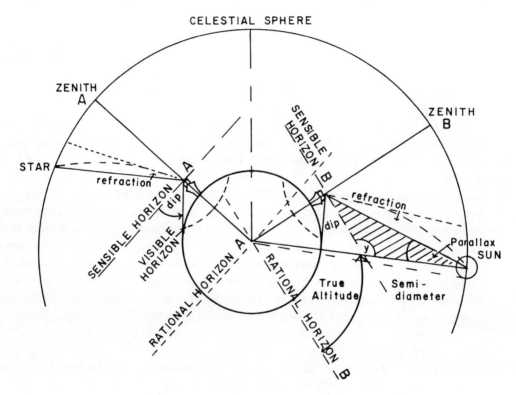

Observer's Visible Horizon

The visible horizon is that bounding the observer's view at sea. The visible horizon of an observer with a height of eye (H.E.) 30 feet above sea level would be at a distance of only about six and one-half miles under normal atmospheric conditions.

The Sensible Horizon

The plane of the sensible horizon passes through the observer's eye and is at right angles to the vertical.

The Rational Horizon

The observer's rational horizon is a great circle, the plane of which is parallel to the sensible horizon and, therefore, at right angles to a line from the Earth's center to the observer's zenith.

Sextant Altitude

The altitude of a body, as observed by sextant, is the angle at the observer between his visible horizon and the body or a limb of the body.

Observed Altitude

The observed altitude of a body is the sextant altitude corrected for any index error which may be present in the sextant.

Dip

The angle of depression of the visible horizon below the sensible horizon is known as dip. Clearly the angle of dip will increase depending on the height of the observer's eye above sea level. A dip table giving values of dip in minutes for the observer's H.E. is contained on the inside cover of the *Nautical Almanac*.

Apparent Altitude

The apparent altitude of a body is the observed altitude corrected for dip. Note that dip will always be *subtracted* from the observed altitude to give the apparent altitude.

Refraction

Rays of light from a body are bent toward the Earth as they pass through layers of varying density in the atmosphere. This tends to make the body appear higher than it actually is; therefore, the correction for refraction is always *subtracted* from the apparent altitude. The correction for refraction diminishes with increased altitude. Values are given, in a correction table for stars and planets, inside the front cover of the *Nautical Almanac*. Altitudes of a body less than about 10° are generally unreliable due to severe refraction.

True Altitude of a Star

The true altitude of a star is the apparent altitude corrected for refraction. The true altitude of any body is, in fact, the angle at the center of the Earth between the observer's rational horizon and the center of the body. In the case of stars, it is only necessary to apply the two corrections of dip and refraction to the observed altitude to obtain the true altitude. With the Sun it is necessary to apply two additional corrections for parallax (see below) and semidiameter in order to obtain the true altitude.

Parallax

Parallax is the angle at the celestial body subtended by the observer and the Earth's center. The value of parallax becomes smaller the farther away from Earth the body is. In the case of stars, parallax is negligible, but for the Moon it becomes as large as one degree. Parallax decreases with altitude and is greatest in value when the body is on the observer's rational horizon. It reduces to zero at a maximum altitude of 90°. The value of parallax at zero altitude is known as horizontal parallax. For the Sun this is about 15″. Intermediate values of parallax can be found by multiplying the horizontal parallax by the cosine of the altitude.

In the diagram of the celestial sphere, for the shaded triangle *by Sun*:

The exterior angle at y = true altitude
Therefore, true altitude = angle B + angle *Sun* (exterior angle of a triangle equals two interior opposite angles)
Therefore, true altitude = apparent altitude (corrected for refraction) + parallax

Note that the parallax correction will always be *added* to the apparent altitude.

Semidiameter

For accuracy and convenience, one measures the altitude of the lower limb of the Sun or Moon rather than attempting to estimate the center of the body. Thus, the semidiameter must be allowed for in order to give the additional arc to the center of the body. Occasionally, it may be necessary to use the upper limb of a body, in which case the measured angle would be too large and the semidiameter would be a *negative* correction.

True Altitude of the Sun

The true altitude of the Sun is the angle at the center of the Earth subtended by the observer's rational horizon and the center of the Sun. The apparent altitude of the Sun when corrected for refraction, parallax, and semidiameter will give the true altitude. These three corrections are combined in a total correction table found on the inside front cover of the *Nautical Almanac*.

True altitude + zenith distance = 90°.

1. Sextant altitude star	1. Sextant altitude Sun's lower	
Index Error ±	limb Index Error ±	
2. Observed altitude Dip −	2. Observed altitude Dip −	
3. Apparent altitude	3. Apparent altitude ⎤	
Refraction −	Refraction −	Total
True altitude star	Parallax + ⎥	Correction
	Semidiameter + ⎦	
	True altitude Sun	

Exercise:
Altitude Correction

Use the altitude correction tables inside the front cover of the *Nautical Almanac*.

1. Find the true altitude of the Pole Star if its sextant atitude was 27° 58′.3 to an observer with a height of eye (H.E.) of 24 feet and the index error (I.E.) was +6′.2.

2. If the sextant altitude of star Rigel was 61° 12′.2 to an observer with H.E. 27.3 feet and I.E. was 2′.3 on the arc, calculate the true altitude.

3. Calculate the true altitude of a star with sextant altitude 19° 15'.2 if the sextant I.E. was 3'.1 off the arc and observer's H.E. was 29 feet.

4. Find the true altitude of Arcturus if its sextant altitude was 81° 15' to an observer with H.E. 32.6 feet and I.E. was 2'.6 off the arc.

5. Find the true altitude of the Sun on March 26, to an observer with H.E. 25.2 feet and I.E. 2'.3 on the arc, if the sextant altitude of ☉ was 26° 31'.5.

6. If the sextant altitude of ☉ was 63° 24'.1 to an observer with H.E. 37 feet and I.E. −2'.1 on January 3, find the true altitude of the Sun.

7. If the sextant altitude of ☉ was 29° 54'.3 to an observer with H.E. 26.1 feet and I.E. was 0'.8 on the arc on June 19, calculate the true altitude of the Sun.

8. The observed altitude of ☉ was 32° 12'.1 to an observer with H.E. 22 feet on January 18. Find the Sun's true altitude.

9. If the sextant altitude of ☉ was 49° 11'.2 to an observer with H.E. 21.6 feet and I.E. was +1'.6, calculate the true altitude if the date was December 12.

10. Find the true altitude of the Sun if the sextant altitude of ☉ was 36° 18' to an observer with H.E. 32 feet and I.E. was 2'.2 on the arc on May 2. State the true zenith distance of the Sun.

34

LATITUDE BY MERIDIAN ALTITUDE

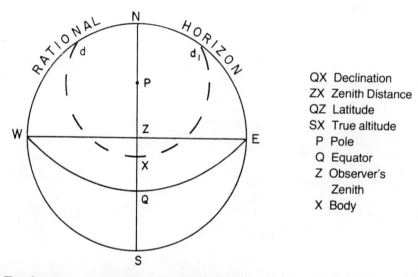

QX Declination
ZX Zenith Distance
QZ Latitude
SX True altitude
 P Pole
 Q Equator
 Z Observer's
     Zenith
 X Body

As the Earth rotates on its axis each day, any given meridian will come into line with the Sun, Moon, and various stars and planets. It will appear to an observer that these bodies are crossing his meridian from east to west. The apparent path of a body is indicated in the diagram by the dotted circumpolar line dd_1. This is easily drawn with its center at the pole and its radius equal to the complement of the declination (co. dec.). If the exact time of culmination (meridional passage) of a body is known, then its declination (dec.) can be extracted from the *Nautical Almanac,* and thus the body can be located on the observer's meridian relative to the equator.

A true altitude of a body, taken at time of meridian passage, and subtracted from 90° will give the angular zenith distance of the observer's zenith from the body. Thus a combination of zenith distance and declination will give the observer's latitude. Four examples of latitude by meridian altitude follow. *Note that the diagrams are drawn in the plane of the observer's rational horizon with the observer's zenith at the center.* This simple method of latitude determination is commonly used at local apparent noon when the Sun reaches its zenith, crossing the observer's meridian either to his north or to his south.

When a body is on the observer's meridian, its local hour angle (L.H.A.) is zero. The Greenwich hour angle (G.H.A.) of the body can be found by applying the observer's longitude to the zero L.H.A., and the exact time of meridional passage can then be calculated easily by extracting the Greenwich mean time (G.M.T.) that matches this G.H.A. in the *Nautical Almanac*.

The G.M.T. of meridian passage at Greenwich for Sun, Moon, Aries, and the planets is given to the nearest minute at the bottom of each page in the *Nautical Almanac*. The observer's longitude in time is applied to this figure to give the approximate Greenwich time of local meridian passage of the body concerned. Latitude by meridian altitude is used less often for stars because the time of meridian altitude must then coincide with the few minutes of twilight time that both the star and a clear horizon can be seen.

Example 1.

Given true meridian altitude of Sun 35°20′ bearing south with declination 20°10′N, calculate the observer's latitude.

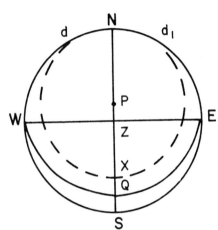

ZX, the zenith distance $= 90° - 35°20′$
$$= 54°40′$$
QX, the declination $\quad = 20°10′N$
Therefore, equator Q is 20°10′ south of the body.
The observer's latitude $= ZQ = QX + ZX$
Therefore, latitude = 74-50N.

Example 2.

Given true meridian altitude of Sun 48°18′ bearing north of the observer with declination 03°15′S, calculate the observer's latitude.

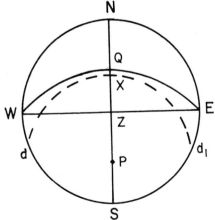

ZX, the zenith distance $= 90° - 48°18′$
$$= 41°42′$$
QX, the declination $\quad = 03°15′S$
Therefore, equator Q is 03°15′ north of the body.
The observer's latitude $= ZQ = QX + ZX$
Therefore, latitude = 44-57S.

Example 3.

Calculate the latitude of an observer with longitude 000°00' on August 26, 1968, if the true meridian altitude of the Sun was 43°12' bearing south.

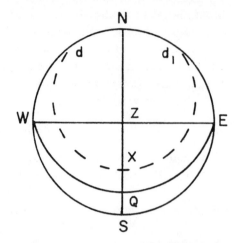

ZX, the zenith distance = 90° − 43°12'

$\qquad\qquad\qquad\qquad = 46°48'$

From *Nautical Almanac* for August 26, G.M.T. of sun's meridian passage at Greenwich is 12h02m and declination is 10-18N.

From diagram latitude QZ = QX + ZX

$\qquad\qquad\qquad\qquad = 57\text{-}06N$

Therefore, latitude = 57-06N.

Exact time of passage is when L.H.A. = zero.

In this case, L.H.A. = G.H.A. as longitude = zero.

G.H.A. = 359°34'.4 at 1200 and, therefore, requires 00°25'.6 until noon.

The increment tables give the equivalent time of 1m42s.

Therefore, G.M.T. of apparent noon = 12h01m42s.

Example 4.

Calculate the latitude of an observer in longitude 022-15W if the true meridian altitude of the Sun was 57°05' bearing north of the observer on August 27, 1968.

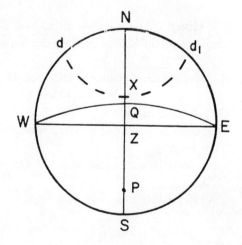

ZX, the zenith distance = 90° − 57°05'

$\qquad\qquad\qquad\qquad = 32°55'$

From *Nautical Almanac* for August 27, G.M.T. of sun's meridian passage of Greenwich = 1201

Therefore, G.M.T. will be 22°15' of time later on the observer's meridian

Therefore, G.M.T. of local passage of the Sun = 1201 + 1h29m

G.M.T. of passage = 1330

Therefore, dec. of the Sun = 09°55.6'N

$\qquad\qquad = QX.$

From the diagram, latitude QZ = ZX − QX

Therefore, latitude = 22-59.4S.

Exact time of passage is when L.H.A. = zero.

As longitude is 022-15W then if L.H.A.
  = zero, G.H.A. = 22°15'.
G.H.A. = 14°38'.8 at 1300, leaving
  22°15' − 14°38'.8 until local noon.
The increment tables give the equivalent time of 30m25s.
Therefore, G.M.T. of apparent noon =
  13h30m25s.

Exercise:
Meridian Altitudes

Draw a diagram in the plane of the observer's rational horizon for each question.

1. Determine the latitude of an observer if the sun's true meridian altitude was 67°13' with a declination of 18-22S, bearing north of the observer.

2. Find the latitude of an observer when the true altitude of the Sun, bearing north, was 37°22' with a declination of 07-15N.

3. The true meridian altitude of the Sun bearing south was 67°22' when the Sun's declination was 11-18S. Find the latitude of the observer.

4. The minimum shadow cast by a 6-foot pole was exactly 6 feet on June 21. Find the approximate latitude of the observer without the use of tables or the *Nautical Almanac*. The observer was south of the Sun.

5. Determine the latitude of an observer if the sextant altitude of the ☉ at local apparent noon was 23°28'.5 bearing south. The I.E. was 2'.4 on the arc, H.E. 24 feet, and declination of the Sun, 22-18S.

6. Calculate the latitude of an observer in longitude 0°00' on August 25, 1968, if the true meridian altitude of the Sun was 42°22' bearing south.

7. Determine the latitude of an observer in longitude 078-20W on August 27, 1968, if the true meridian altitude of the Sun was 84°06' bearing south.

8. Find the latitude of an observer in longitude 062-15E if the observed altitude of ☉ was 70°10'.3 on August 26, 1968. The observer's H.E. was 27 feet, and the apparent sun crossed his meridian bearing south.

9. State the exact Greenwich time of meridian passage of the Sun and the observer's latitude if the sun's true altitude at this time was 36°27' bearing north. The observer's longitude was 038-05W and the date was August 25, 1968.

10. Calculate the exact local time of meridian passage of the Sun and the observer's latitude if the observed altitude of ☉ at the time was 74°38'.6 bearing south. The observer's longitude was 065-12E, his H.E. 29 feet, and the date was August 27, 1968.

35

AZIMUTH AND AMPLITUDE

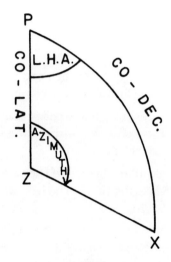

Time Azimuth

The azimuth of a body is the angle at the observer's zenith contained between the observer's meridian and the vertical circle passing through the body concerned.

In the pole-body-zenith spherical triangle (*PZX*), it is possible to calculate the azimuth angle *PZX*, providing two sides and an included angle are known. If Greenwich time is observed upon taking a compass bearing of a body, then figures for an accurate local hour angle and the declination of the body can be extracted from the *Nautical Almanac*. The declination is then either added or subtracted from 90° to give the co-dec., or polar distance, side of the triangle. An estimated latitude, when subtracted from 90°, will provide the other side of the triangle, and the angle between these two sides will be the L.H.A.

Tables based on arguments of latitude, declination, and hour angle preclude the necessity for solving the *PZX* triangle by trigonometry, and the true azimuth can be readily extracted from such tables in a few seconds.

Thus, a comparison of the true and compass azimuths of a certain body will yield the compass error at any instant. This method of determining compass error should be regularly practiced and carried out after each alteration of course if possible. The actual compass bearing of the body is obtained by observing the Sun through an azimuth mirror. The azimuth mirror has a ring which is mounted over the compass and is free to turn. The ring bears a glass prism through which a body may be observed while looking at the compass card graduation.

Various tables are available and the following exercise may be worked with whichever set of tables the navigator has available. The following example is worked with the tables in H.O. Pub. No. 229.

Example 1.

Calculate the true bearing of the Sun on August 26, 1968, to an observer in latitude 32-24N longitude 023-00W at 1430 L.M.T. If the compass bearing of the Sun was 260° C at this time, what is the compass error?

Step 1.

Determine G.M.T. and extract G.H.A. and dec. from the *Nautical Almanac.*

L.M.T.	14h30m
Long. in time	1h32m
G.M.T.	16h02m
G.H.A. 16h	59°35'.1
Increment 02m	0°30'
G.H.A.	60°05'.1
Dec.	10°14'.5N

Step 2.

Apply longitude to G.H.A. to obtain L.H.A. Convert L.H.A. to meridian angle (t) where necessary.

G.H.A.	60°	05'.1	
Long.	23°	00'W	*Note: Longitude west G.H.A. best;*
L.H.A.	37°	05'.1	*Longitude east G.H.A. least.*

Step 3.

With the three arguments of meridian angle, declination, and latitude, enter the sight reduction tables and interpolate for azimuth angle as shown below.

	t	d	L
Data	37.1W	10.2N	32.4N
Base / Z	37 / 114.5	10 / 114.5	32 / 114.5
Next / Z	38 / 113.5	11 / 113.2	33 / 115.5
Difference	− 1.0	− 1.3	+1.0
Multiplier	(0.1)	(0.2)	(0.4)
Product	−0.10	−0.26	+0.40
			−0.36
Sum			+0.04

Result   Z = N 114.54 W yielding Zn = 245.5° T
                                          = 260.0° C
                             CE = 014.5 W

Example 2.

The following data are taken by the navigator of a vessel in D.R. 41-23.4S, 070-45.6W on August 26, 1968. G.M.T. = 13-27-30; compass bearing of Sun = 063.7° C; local variation = 11.5 W. What is the deviation of the compass?

$$
\begin{aligned}
\text{(13 h) G.H.A.} &= 014\text{-}34.6 & \text{(13 h) d} &= \text{N } 10\text{-}17.2 \\
\text{(27-30) increment} &= \underline{6\text{-}52.5} & \text{(.9) cor'n} &= \underline{.4\,\text{S}} \\
\text{Final G.H.A.} &= 021\text{-}27.1 & \text{final d} &= \text{N } 10\text{-}16.8 \\
\text{D.R. longitude} &= \underline{070\text{-}45.6\text{W}} & & \\
\text{(L.H.A.} &= 310\text{-}41.5) & & \\
t &= 049\text{-}18.5\text{E} & &
\end{aligned}
$$

	t	d	L
Data	49.3 E	10.3 N	41.4 S
Base / Z	49 / 126.7	10 / 126.7	41 / 126.7
Next / Z	50 / 125.9	11 / 127.4	42 / 127.1
Difference	− 0.8	+ 0.7	+ 0.4
Multiplier	(0.3)	(0.3)	(0.4)
Product	− 0.24	+ 0.21	+0.16
	+ 0.37		
Sum	+ 0.13		
Result	Z = S 126.83 E, yielding Zn = 053.2 °T		

$$
\begin{aligned}
\theta &= \underline{063.7\ \text{°C}} \\
\text{CE} &= 10.5\ \text{W} \\
\text{Var.} &= \underline{11.5\ \text{W}} \\
\text{Dev.} &= 1.0\ \text{E}
\end{aligned}
$$

Amplitudes

The bearing amplitude of a body is the arc of the horizon contained between east and a rising body or between west and a setting body. The usual 360° notation of bearings refers to north; the older quadrantal system refers to north and south, but the amplitude uses east and west as its origin.

The diagram shows the path of body X with a northerly declination, dXd_1, and the path of body Y, with a southerly declination, DYD_1. Thus, the amplitude of body X rising is angle EZd and the amplitude of body Y rising is angle EZD. The amplitude of bodies X and Y setting would be angle WZd_1 and angle WZD_1, respectively. Clearly a body will always rise and set on a northerly bearing when its declination is north, and will rise and set on a southerly bearing when its declination is south. The amplitude, therefore, is always named the same as the body's declination.

Finding the amplitude of the Sun is a quick and simple method of determining compass error. Theoretical sunrise occurs when the center of the Sun is on the observer's rational horizon. However, refraction, which is maximum at zero altitude, makes the Sun appear to rise about 33 minutes above the horizon when it is theoretically at an altitude of zero degrees. This value of 33 minutes roughly corresponds to the diameter of the Sun; to allow for this, amplitudes should be taken when the Sun's center is about the Sun's diameter clear of the horizon. In other words, there should be

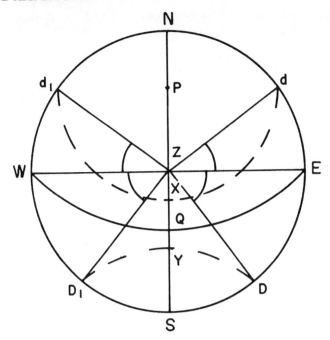

a clearance about the Sun's semidiameter between the horizon and the Sun's lower limb at the time of amplitude. A table is provided in Bowditch's *American Practical Navigator* for correction of amplitudes as observed on the visible horizon.

The true amplitude may be calculated from the formula: Sine amplitude = sine declination × secant latitude. This formula is deduced from Napier's Rules for the solution of right-angled spherical triangles. These rules will be discussed later in the text.

The problem is much more readily solved by extracting the true amplitude directly from prepared amplitude tables. Most sets of nautical tables contain an amplitude table which is based on the above formula and which requires no detailed explanation on its use. The table is merely entered with the arguments of latitude and declination to give the amplitude bearing.

The L.M.T. of sunrise and sunset for any observer is listed in the *Nautical Almanac* for certain latitudes at 3-day intervals. One must interpolate between the listed latitudes in order to obtain an accurate time of sunrise or sunset in intermediate latitudes.

Exercise:
Time Azimuths

1. Determine the true azimuth of the Sun at 0900 G.M.T. to an observer in latitude 39-00N, longitude 000° 00' on August 26, 1968.

2. What is the true bearing of the Sun at Z.T. = 11-30-48 (Z.D. = −1) to an observer in dead reckoning (D.R.) position 36-02N, 014-48E on August 25, 1968?

3. Calculate the Sun's true azimuth if its declination was 12-30S to an observer in D.R. position 38-12N, 077-18W. The G.H.A. of the Sun was 128°57'.

4. Find the true bearing of the Sun at 1740 G.M.T. on August 27, 1968, if the observer's D.R. position was 30-12S, 032-15W.

5. What was the true azimuth of the Sun at 0940 G.M.T. to an observer in D.R. position 42-10N, 045-18W on August 25, 1968?

6. Calculate the compass error of a vessel in D.R. position 38-12N, 037-42W if the Sun bearing 070° C at 0850 G.M.T. on August 26,1968.

7. What was the true azimuth of star Arcturus on August 25, 1968, at 2030 G.M.T. if the observer was in an estimated postion of 45-00N, 008-06W?

8. An observer in D.R. position 34-12S, 135-08W observed the Sun bearing 090° C. If the declination of the Sun was 08-20S and its G.H.A. was 94°17', find the compass error.

9. If the G.H.A. of Aries was 325°18' to an observer in latitude 36-15N, longitude 165-12E, and star Sirius was bearing 195° C, calculate the compass error. The declination of Sirius was 16-40S and its S.H.A. was 259°3'.8.

10. Calculate the deviation of the compass at G.M.T. = 11-09-12 on August 27, if the Sun was bearing 107° C to an observer in latitude 30-12N, longitude 057-18W. The variation was 17°W.

Exercise:
Amplitudes

1. Calculate the amplitude of the Sun if it set with a declination of 10-30S to an observer in latitude 29-00N.

2. Calculate the azimuth of the Sun if it rose with a declination 17-12N to an observer in latitude 49-15N.

3. What would be the setting amplitude of the Sun on June 21, 1968, to an observer in latitude 39-24N? If the Sun was bearing 284° C at this time, what was the compass error?

4. Determine the approximate amplitude of the Sun at time of setting on September 22, 1968.

5. Find the compass error if the Sun rose bearing 090° C to an observer in position 45-06N, 035-10W on August 26, 1968.

36

THE POLE STAR

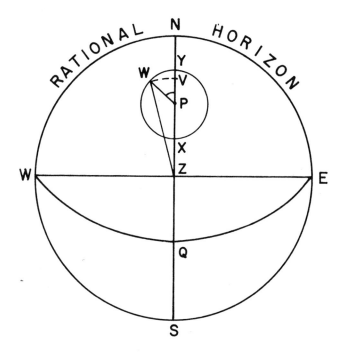

In the above diagram, *NP*, the altitude of the celestial pole, will *always* equal *ZQ*, the latitude of the observer. *NZ* equals 90° and *QP* equals 90°; therefore, as the latitude changes, so do the positions of *Q* in the diagram and *P* by the same account. Thus *NP* equals *ZQ*.

If there were a star situated exactly at the celestial pole, its true altitude would always represent the observer's latitude. Unfortunately, there is no such star, but the star Polaris is sufficiently close to the pole for its altitude to be used to find the observer's latitude after making three minor corrections.

The apparent motion of all stars is circumpolar due to the effect of the rotation of Earth. The Pole Star, as Polaris is known, appears to perform a small circle about the celestial pole, never moving more than about 2° in azimuth east or west of north. As the earth rotates daily, the Pole Star will cross the observer's meridian twice. The *upper meridian passage* occurs when the body is on the meridian between the observer's zenith and the pole (*X* in the diagram). The *lower meridian passage* occurs when the body crosses the observer's meridian on the farther side of the pole at *Y*.

The observer's latitude can be obtained by observation of the Pole Star at any time both the star and a clear horizon are visible. The true altitude of the Pole Star is corrected by an amount equal to *VP* in the diagram where *ZW* equals *ZV* equals the zenith distance.

Thus, true altitude ± correction = latitude.

Clearly, from the diagram, the correction should be *added* to the altitude when the Pole Star is north of an east-west line from the pole and *subtracted* from the altitude when the Pole Star is south of an east-west line from the pole.

However, to avoid confusion the *Pole Star tables* contain a total of 1° in constants in order to keep the three necessary corrections always positive. The 1° is subtracted afterwards.

Therefore, from the Pole Star tables

Latitude = true altitude of Pole Star + a_0 + a_1 + a_2 −1°

The Pole Star tables are contained in the back of the *Nautical Almanac* and one page of these tables is reproduced in the appendix. (Note the illustration at the bottom of that page.) The following exercise can be worked from this.

Exercise:
Pole Star

1. Calculate the latitude of an observer in longitude 052-15W when the sextant altitude of the Pole Star, out of the meridian, was 43°17'. The G.H.A. of Aries was 249°45', the observer's H.E. 15 feet, I.E. 2'.0 on the arc and the month June.

2. On August 25, 1968, at 0540 G.M.T. in longitude 108-14E, the sextant altitude of Polaris, out of the meridian, was 34°52', I.E. 1'.7 off the arc, and H.E. 23 feet. Find the latitude.

3. The observed altitude of the Pole Star, out of the meridian, on August 27, 1968, at 1946 G.M.T., was 53°18'. The observer's longitude was 048-32W and his H.E. 23 feet. Calculate the latitude.

4. Determine the latitude of an observer in longitude 137-45W, when the sextant altitude of Polaris, out of the meridian, was 47°22', I.E. 2'.1 on the arc, H.E. 14 feet. The G.H.A. of Aries was 5°23' and the month was December.

5. On August 26, 1968, at 03h22m13s by chronometer in longitude 099-23E, the sextant altitude of the Pole Star, out of the meridian, was 66°52'. The chronometer was 16m15s fast and the observer's H.E. 25 feet. At this time the Pole Star was bearing 348° C. Calculate the latitude of the observer and the compass error.

37

THE CELESTIAL POSITION LINE

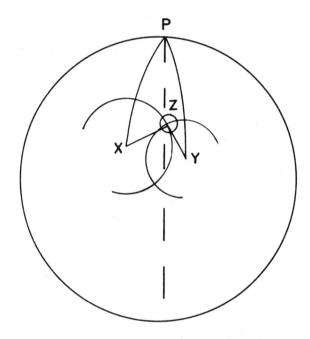

The true zenith distance (T.Z.D.) of a body provides the radius of a position circle centered at the geographical position of the body at the instant of observation. Simultaneous observations of two bodies will provide two such position circles, radii XZ and ZY in the diagram. The observer will be at one of the two intersections of the position circles, and it will be obvious, by consulting the azimuth of the bodies, which intersection is the observer's true position. At position Z, as marked in the diagram, body X should be bearing about west, while body Y will have an azimuth of about south by east.

Unfortunately, such a method of plotting a vessel's position does not provide sufficiently accurate results to be of practical use. The chart plotting sheet would need to be very small scale to take such large position circles, and small errors in construction would result in large discrepancies in positions.

Only the small section of arc in the vicinity of the observer's predicted position needs to be drawn when determining it from position circles. If the zenith distance is not too small, this arc can be considered a straight line with no appreciable error. It can easily be seen from the preceding diagram that such a straight position line will be perpendicular to the azimuth of the body. The problem is to be able to plot this position line without working from its center of origin. To do this, the altitude intercept method of plotting celestial position lines is most commonly used.

The Altitude Intercept Method

To plot the celestial position line by the intercept method, the celestial triangle *PZX* is solved for an assumed latitude and longitude to give a calculated zenith distance for these conditions. Any difference between the calculated zenith distance (C.Z.D.) and the T.Z.D., as observed, will be the error of the assumed position in a direction either toward or away from the bearing of the body.

This will perhaps be more easily understood by comparing a result from the intercept method with an estimate of a distance off a light corrected by an accurate distance off by radar.

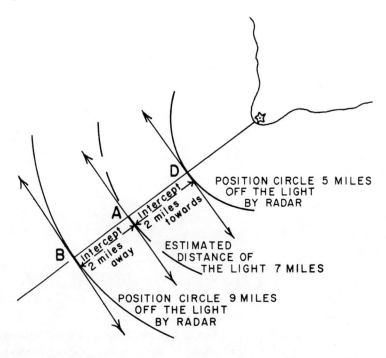

In the above diagram, the lighthouse is bearing northeast and the skipper assumes his distance offshore to be seven miles by "guesstimate" only. If the radar indicates that he is in fact only five miles off the lighthouse, his actual position can be found by measuring off an intercept *AD* two miles toward the lighthouse along the bearing. If the radar had indicated a distance offshore of nine miles, the position could be located by measuring off an intercept *AB* of two miles away from the assumed position.

This system is employed with celestial position lines. If the T.Z.D. is *smaller* than the C.Z.D., the intercept is laid off by that amount *toward* the bearing of the body and the position line drawn through this point perpendicular to the bearing. If the T.Z.D. is *larger* than the C.Z.D., then the intercept is laid off by that amount *away* from, or directly opposite the bearing of the body, and the position line is drawn through this point perpendicular to the bearing.

Example

A vessel in D.R. 42-20N, 035-15W observes the Sun with a True Altitude of 60°10′ bearing southeast. The Sun's C.Z.D. as calculated from the spherical *PZX* triangle, using the above D.R. position, was 29°46′. State a position through which to draw the position line.

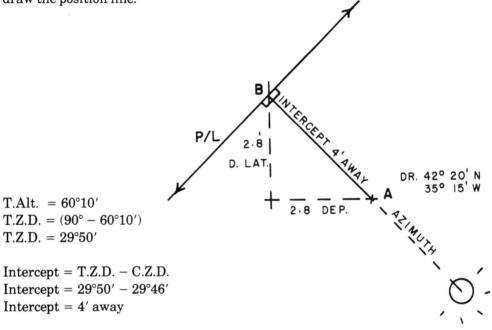

T.Alt. = 60°10′
T.Z.D. = (90° − 60°10′)
T.Z.D. = 29°50′

Intercept = T.Z.D. − C.Z.D.
Intercept = 29°50′ − 29°46′
Intercept = 4′ away

1. The intercept AB is constructed to scale, away from the D.R. position, in the direction opposite the azimuth.

2. The position line is laid off at the end of the intercept, perpendicular to the line of bearing.

3. The departure (dep.) and difference of latitude (d. lat.) of position *B* from position *A* are determined by scale measurement.

4. Dep. is converted to difference of longitude (d. long.) by the traverse tables or by the formula:

$$\text{Dep.} = \text{DLo} \times \text{cosine mean lat.}$$

5. D. lat. and d. long. are applied to the D.R. position to give the intercept terminal position *B*. In the diagram the 4′ intercept is drawn away from the bearing toward the northwest. The position line is drawn from northeast to southwest through the intercept terminal position (I.T.P.). The d. lat. 2′.8 and dep. 2′.8 are taken off as to the scale, and the dep. is converted to d. long. to give 3′.8.

	D.R. position	42-20 N	035-15 W
	l 2.8N		DLo 3.8W
	I.T.P.	42-22.8N	035-18.8W

Therefore, to be able to use the intercept method of plotting position lines we require T.Z.D., azimuth, and C.Z.D. The T.Z.D. is easily found by subtracting the true altitude from 90° (see Exercise 3), and the azimuth is found by tables (see Exercise 5). Calculation of the C.Z.D. is more complicated but is easily done with a little practice.

Solving the *PZX* triangle to yield the C.Z.D. can be accomplished in three different ways: (1) trigonometric calculation, (2) short method tables, or (3) inspection tables. Theory and examples on the first two methods follow, but we will be more concerned with the practical use of the third.

38

THREE METHODS OF SIGHT REDUCTION

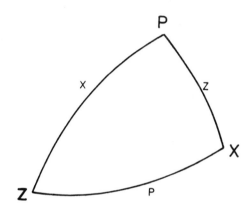

Interior angle at P = meridian angle (t)
Interior angle at Z = azimuth angle (Z)
Interior angle at X = parallactic angle (X)
ZX is p (side opposite P) = zenith distance (z)
PX is z (side opposite Z) = polar distance (p)
PZ is x (side opposite X) = colatitude (co-L)

By Calculation

In 1875 the *altitude intercept method* of determining a position line was intro-duced by a French naval commander named Marcq St.-Hilaire. For about 100 years prior to this, position lines were obtained by the longitude-by-time method made possible by the invention of the chronometer. Various applications of longitude by time or longitude by chronometer are still used by some navigators, possibly due more to habit than to any other reason. However, most navigators prefer the altitude intercept method, and some of these obtain the necessary C.Z.D. by the longer route of calculation rather than by short method tables.

The most popular formulas used for solving the navigational triangle to obtain the calculated zenith distance and calculated azimuth angle are shown below. They are derived from the basic formulas for solution of oblique spherical triangles. The derivations are contained in various other books (e.g., Nicholl's *Concise Guide to Nautical Knowledge,* Vol. II) which have a more theoretical approach to the subject.

To find the calculated zenith distance (z), the cosine-haversine formula is used:

$$\text{hav } z = \text{hav} (L \sim d) + \cos L \cos d \text{ hav } t$$

where hav means haversine and is positive whether the angle is positive or negative; z is calculated zenith distance; L is D.R. or assumed latitude; ~ means absolute difference without regard to the sign of the *answer*; d is the declination; and t is the meridian angle.

To find the calculated azimuth angle (Z), the sine formula is used:

$$\sin Z = \sin t \cos d \csc z$$

where Z is azimuth angle, and all other variables are as indicated above.

An example of sight reduction using these formulas follows.

Example

On August 26, 1968, at 0930 L.M.T. the sextant altitude of ☉ was 44°08′.0. The vessel was in D.R. position 39-30N, 071-15W, and the chronometer, which was 9m12s fast of G.M.T., was reading 14h16m41s. Calculate the direction of the position line and a position through which it passes if the observer's H.E. was 16 feet and I.E. was 0′.8 off the arc.

Step 1.

Determine G.M.T. from the chronometer. Check this by making a comparison with local time, having longitude in time applied.

L.M.T.		0930	
Long. in time		445	
Approx. G.M.T.		1415	
Chron.	14h	16m	41s
Error		−9m	12s
G.M.T.	14h	07m	29s

Step 2.

Calculate the L.H.A. by applying longitude to the G.H.A. as extracted from the *Nautical Almanac*. If the L.H.A. exceeds 180° subtract this from 360° to give the meridian angle (t).

G.H.A. 14h	29°	34′.7
Increment	1°	52′.3
G.H.A.	31°	27′
Long.	071°	15′ W
L.H.A.	320°	12′
Angle t	39°	48′ E

Step 3.

Extract declination from the *Nautical Almanac* and then obtain the *difference* from D.R. latitude, if they are of the same name, or the *sum*, if they are of unlike names.

Lat.	39°	30′ N
Dec.	10°	16′.2N
(L ~ d)	29°	13′.8

Step 4.

Correct the sextant altitude and subtract the true altitude from 90° to obtain the T.Z.D.

Sextant alt.	44°	08'.0
I.E.		+'.8
Obs. alt.	44°	08'.8
Dip.		−3'.9
App. alt.	44°	04'.9
T. corr.		+15'.0
T. alt.	44°	19'.9
T.Z.D.	45°	40'.1

Step 5.

Determine the C.Z.D. (z) using the cosine-haversine formula:

$$\text{hav } z = \text{hav } (L{\sim}d) + \cos L \cos d \text{ hav } t.$$

Step 6.

Determine the calculated azmuth angle (Z) using the sine formula:

$$\sin Z = \sin t \cos d \csc z.$$

Then derive the azimuth (Zn) from the azimuth angle.

Nat. hav	No.	Log.
0.06367	hav 29-13.8 = hav (L~d)	
	cos 39-30N = cos L	9.88741
	cos 10-16.2N = cos d	9.99299
	hav 039-48E = hav t	9.06393
0.08797		8.94433
0.15164	hav 45-50.1 = hav z	
	45-40.1 = T.Z.D.	
	10.0 towards	
	sin 039-48E = sin t	9.80625
	(from above) = cos d	9.99299
	csc 45°50'.1 = csc z	10.14428
	sin 61°24'.5 = sin Z	9.94352
	N61.4E = Z	
	061.4 = Zn	

Step 7.

Plot the intercept and azimuth from the D.R. position using some suitable scale. Convert to DLo and apply D. Lat. and DLo to the D.R. position to obtain the I.T.P. From the traverse tables 8'.7 dep. in latitude 39-30N gives 11'.3 DLo.

D.R. position	39°30' N		71°15' W	
D. Lat.	4'.8S	DLo	11'.3E	
I.T.P.: Lat.	39°25'.2N	Long.	71°3'.7W	P.L. 028°.6/208°.6

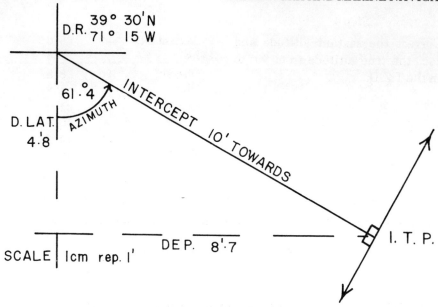

By Short Method Tables

Professional navigators are constantly seeking more rapid and efficient methods of sight reduction. Over the last 50 years many and varied short methods of sight reduction, both mathematical and mechanical, have been devised to satisfy these requirements. Some of these methods are highly complicated and in some cases take just as much time as a calculation. Other methods have been accepted and are used by a few navigators in preference to the inspection method mainly due to the compactness of the tables used.

Some of the more efficient of the short methods divide the celestial *PZX* triangle into two right-angled spherical triangles by having a perpendicular dropped from one angle to the opposite side. Napier's Rules for the solving of right-angled spherical triangles can then be used for sight reduction, and the short method tables can be established, based on a range of conditions already worked and solved by Napier's Rules and presented in tabulated form. A simple explanation of Napier's Rules follows for interested students.

Napier's Rules

The 90° angle is omitted, and the other two angles and the three sides are represented in rotation by a five-part diagram as follows. (Note that the complement (comp.) of the two angles and the complement of the hypotenuse side are used.)

Providing that the values of any two of the five sections in the diagram are known, the other three can be found by the following formulae:

Sine of a part = product of tangents of adjacent parts
Sine of a part = product of cosines or opposite parts

Adjacent part means the one next to, and opposite part means the one past adjacent. If, for example, side *c* and angle *B* are known and *C* is required

$$\sin \text{comp. } C = \cos c \times \cos \text{comp. } B,$$
$$\cos C = \cos c \times \sin B$$

If a is required

$$\sin \text{comp. } B = \tan c \times \tan \text{comp. } a, \text{ and transposing}$$
$$\cot a = \cos B \times \cot c$$

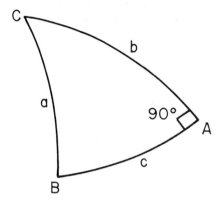
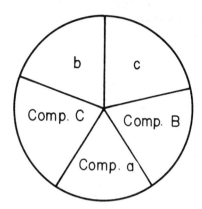

Care must be taken with the *rule of signs* and various special cases which arise using this method. For a detailed explanation refer to *Spherical Trigonometry* by J. H. Clough-Smith.

Following is the only short method table to be examined in this text with a brief explanation and example of the Ageton method, using publication H.O. No. 211, *Ageton's Short Method Tables.*

Ageton Short Method Table

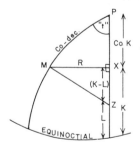

The celestial triangle, in this case triangle *PMZ*, is divided into two right-angled spherical triangles by dropping a perpendicular from the body *M* to meet the observer's meridian at *X*.

In the right triangle *PMX*, t, the meridian angle, and *PM*, the co-dec. of the body, are both known. Therefore, R and Co-K, easily found by Napier's Rules, are then links, or auxiliaries, for use in the second right triangle *MXZ*.

The D.R. latitude L is subtracted from K to give the side (K ~ L) in right triangle *MXZ*. Thus, finding the value of R and (K ~ L), through Napier's Rules, side *MZ* in the triangle *MXZ* can be found. *MZ* is the calculated zenith distance which, when subtracted from the true zenith distance, provides the intercept.

To make these tables easier to use, all formulae are converted to the form of secants and cosecants which are multiplied by 100,000 for simplified presentation.

This method provides the result of the sight reduction as the calculated altitude (Hc), which, when subtracted from the true altitude (Ho), gives the intercept. Of course, in this case, the intercept is measured *toward* the azimuth from the D.R. position because Ho is larger than Hc. A number of examples are provided in the front of H.O. 211, Ageton, but how to use the table will become apparent after working a few examples. The previous example of sight reduction by calculation is worked below by the Ageton method.

Example

On August 26, 1968, at 0930 L.M.T. the sextant altitude of ☉ was 44°08'.0. The vessel was in D.R. position 39-30N, 071-15W and the chronometer, which was 9m12s fast of G.M.T., was reading 14h16m41s. Calculate the direction of the position line and a position through which it passes if the observer's H.E. was 16 feet and I.E. 0'.8 off the arc.

Step 1.

Determine G.M.T. from the chronometer. Check this by making a comparison with local time, having longitude in time applied.

L.M.T.			0930
Long. in time			445
Approx. G.M.T.			1415
Chron.	14h	16m	41s
Error		− 9m	12s
G.M.T.	14h	07m	29s

Step 2.

Calculate the L.H.A. by applying longitude to the G.H.A. as extracted from the *Nautical Almanac*. If the L.H.A. exceeds 180° subtract this from 360° to give the meridian angle t.

G.H.A. 14h	29°	34'.7
Increment	1°	52'.3
G.H.A.	31°	27'
Long.	071°	15'W
L.H.A.	320°	12'
Angle t	39°	48'E

Step 3.

Correct the sextant altitude.

Dec.	10°	16'.2N
Sex. alt.	44°	08'.0
I.E.		+ 0'.8
Obs. alt.	44°	08'.8
Dip		− 3'.9
App. alt.	44°	04'.9
T. Corr.		+15'.0
T. alt.	44°	19'.9

		Add	Subtract	Add	Subtract
Angle t	39°48'.0E	A 19,375			
Dec.	10°16'.2N	B 701	A 74,888		
R		A 20,076	B 10,974	B 10,974	A 20,076
K	13°16'.2N		A 63,914		
D.R. L	39°30' N				
(K~L)	26°13'.8			B 4,721	
Hc	44° 9'.8			A 15,695	B 14,427
Ho	44°19'.9				A 5,649
Int.	10'.1	towards			ZS61°24'E
					Zn 118.6

Step 4.

Enter tables with meridian angle t, and take out the number from column A. Enter tables with declination and take out the number from the column B. Add these two numbers to give the R value.

Step 5.

Look up the number obtained from step 4 in column A and take out the number beside it in column B. Subtract this from the A function of declination as extracted from the tables.

Step 6.

With the number obtained from step 5, take out the nearest tabulated value of K from the tables and give it the same name as the declination. Combine K with the D.R. latitude to obtain (K~L). Add K and L if their names are *different*; *subtract* the smaller from the larger if they are *alike*.

Step 7.

Enter table with (K~L) value and extract the B value from the table. Add this to the B function of R. Enter the table with this number and extract Hc. The difference between Hc (computed altitude) and Ho (true altitude) will be the intercept. The intercept will be *toward* the body from the D.R. position when Ho is larger than Hc.

Step 8.

Look up Hc in the B column and subtract this from the A function of R which was determined in step 1. With this number enter the A column and take out the azimuth to the nearest minute. The intercept and azimuth are then plotted in exactly the same manner as used in the calculation method.

Note: The short method of sight reduction may appear as anything but that when first examined by the student. However, when the tables have been used a number of times and a few obvious shortcuts have been applied, it will be found to be somewhat quicker to use than the calculation method.

By Inspection Tables

Inspection tables are lists of altitudes and azimuths computed from navigational triangles at standard intervals. It is obvious that as the latitude, the hour angle, or the declination of a celestial triangle changes, then so must the azimuth and the altitude. Modern inspection tables provide instant readouts of azimuth and altitude when entered with the three arguments of latitude, declination, and local hour angle. The latitude and hour angle are listed for every single degree and the declination, for each half degree. Intermediate arguments between degrees can be used by interpolation. A table is provided to facilitate this.

Tables of Computed Altitude and Azimuth was first published during the Second World War by the U. S. Navy Hydrographic Office as H.O. Pub. No. 214. The need for such tables had long been obvious, but it was not until the advent of the computer that their construction became feasible. H.O. Pub. No. 214 consists of nine volumes, each covering a range of 10° of latitude. It is only because of the relative unwieldiness of nine volumes that some mariners prefer using some of the more compact short method tables.

H.O. Pub. No. 214 was replaced on December 31, 1975, by H.O. Pub. No. 229. The new publication entitled *Sight Reduction Tables for Marine Navigation* consists of six volumes which provide the navigator with a method of more precise sight reduction and positioning than ever before possible. These inspection tables provide the quickest and simplest method of sight reduction and are recommended to the budding navigator.

Two stages of interpolation can be avoided by using an assumed position rather than a D.R. position. The assumed position will always have a latitude to the nearest whole degree of the D.R. latitude and a longitude that, when applied to the G.H.A., will provide an L.H.A. reduced to whole degrees only. Thus the only argument requiring interpolation is that of declination. It is emphasized that this feature is made possible by use of the altitude intercept method of determining a position line; due care should be taken when plotting the position line from assumed position.

The previous example is now reworked, using H.O. Pub. No. 229. An exercise follows. Worked examples and description of the tables are in the front of each volume of H.O. Pub. No. 229.

Example

On August 26, 1968, at Z.T. 1007, the sextant altitude of ☉ was 44°8′.0. The vessel was in D.R. position 39-30N, 071-15W and the chronometer, which was 9m12s fast of G.M.T., was reading 14h16m41s. Calculate the direction of the position line and a position through which it passes if the observer's H.E. was 16 feet and the I.E. was 0′.8 off the arc.

Step 1.

Determine G.M.T. from the chronometer. Check this against zone time (Z.T. = G.M.T. − Z.D.).

$$
\begin{array}{rrrr}
\text{C.T.} = & 14 & 16 & 41 \\
\text{C.E. (fast)} = & & 09 & 12 \\
\hline
\text{G.M.T.} = & 14 & 07 & 29 \\
\text{Z.D. (E.D.T.)} = & +4 & & \\
\hline
\text{Z.T.} = & 10 & - & 07
\end{array}
$$

Step 2.

Determine G.H.A. and d from the *Almanac*.

$$
\begin{aligned}
(14\,h)\ \text{G.H.A.} &= 029\text{-}34.7 \\
(07\text{-}29)\ \text{increment} &= \underline{\ \ 01\text{-}52.2} \\
\text{final G.H.A.} &= 031\text{-}26.9 \\
\text{assumed long.} &= \underline{071\text{-}26.9\text{W}} \\
t &= 040\text{-}00.0\text{E} \\
(\text{L.H.A.} &= 320\text{-}00.0)
\end{aligned}
$$

Step 3.

Determine L.H.A. (as necessary) and t by assuming a longitude which will yield L.H.A. and t in whole degrees.

$$
\begin{aligned}
d &= \text{N } 10\text{-}16.3 \\
(.9)\ \text{cor'n} &= \underline{\ \ \ \ 0.1\,\text{S}} \\
\text{final } d &= \text{N } 10\text{-}16.2
\end{aligned}
$$

Step 4.

Correct the sextant altitude.

$$
\begin{aligned}
\text{Hs} &= 44\text{-}08.0 \\
\text{I.E. \& dip} &= \underline{\ \ -3.1} \\
\text{Ha} &= 44\text{-}04.9 \\
\text{main} &= \underline{\ +15.0} \\
\text{Ho} &= 44\text{-}19.9
\end{aligned}
$$

Step 5.

Enter the inspection tables (sight reduction tables) to determine the calculated altitude and azimuth.

Arguments	Solution
t = 40 E	Hc = 44-15.9
d = N 10-16.2	Z = N 118.2 E
L = 39 N	Zn = 118.2

Step 6.

Determine the altitude intercept and azimuth.

$$
\begin{aligned}
\text{Ho} &= 44\text{-}19.9\ (\text{from Step 4}) \\
\text{Hc} &= 44\text{-}15.9\ (\text{from Step 5}) \\
a &= \quad 4.0\ \text{towards Zn} = 118.2
\end{aligned}
$$

Step 7.

Plot the line of position (L.O.P.). This requires laying down a bearing line through the *assumed* position in the direction of the azimuth; measuring the altitude intercept from that assumed position along the bearing line *towards* or *away from* that assumed position; and, at this distance from the assumed position, drawing the L.O.P. perpendicular to the bearing line.

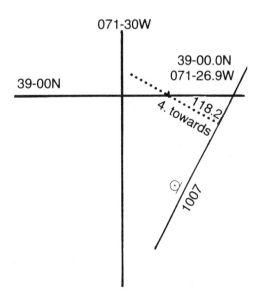

Notice that a and Zn here are slightly different from those determined by the previous two methods. This is because an assumed position rather than a D.R. position was used here. The line of position thus achieved, however, will be indistinguishable from those achieved by calculation or short method tables.

Exercise:
Sight Reduction

Work each problem by all three methods to learn the advantages and disadvantages of each method.

1. A vessel in D.R. position 38-18N, 042-15W had a corrected chronometer reading of 11h08m15s on August 27, 1968, when the true altitude of the Sun was 32°57'.4. Calculate the direction of the position line and a position through which it passes.

2. Calculate the direction of the position line and a position through which it passes if the observed altitude of the ☉ was 41°26' when the G.H.A. of the Sun was 96°36' with a declination of 10-47S. The vessel was in D.R. position 32-08N, 073-46W with an H.E. of 15 feet.

3. The true altitude of the Sun was 31°10' to a vessel in D.R. position 36-20N, 052-36W when the G.H.A. of the Sun was 117°23'. Calculate the direction of the position line and a position through which it passes if the Sun's declination at this time was 18-54N.

4. On August 25, 1968, the true altitude of the Sun was 38°11'.6 to a vessel in D.R. position 35-18N, 064-57W. The chronometer, which was 7m12s fast of G.M.T., read 13h06m48s. Find the direction of the position line and a position through which it passes.

5. Determine the direction of the position line and a position through which it passes if the observed altitude of ☉ was 21°01' to an observer in D.R. position 31-02N, 125-07E. The G.H.A. of the Sun was 285°15' and its declination was 17-54S. The observer's H.E. was 19 feet.

6. On August 26, 1968, at Z.T. = 1007 the sextant altitude ☉ was 53°08'. The vessel was in D.R. position 33-42N, 047-18W and the chronometer, which was 6m42s slow of G.M.T., was reading 13h00m14s. Calculate the direction of the position line and a position through which it passes if the observer's H.E. was 17 feet and the I.E. was 1'.2 on the arc.

7. The true altitude of star Sirius was 19°35' when its G.H.A. was 100°17'. Calculate the direction of the position line and a position through which it passes if the observer was in D.R. position 32-47N, 048-18W.

8. On August 27, 1968, the observed altitude of star Pollux was 37°25'.5 when the corrected chronometer reading was 08h08m40s. Determine the direction of the position line and a position through which it passes if the vessel was in D.R. position 37-14N, 044-48W. The observer's H.E. was 20 feet.

9. Calculate the direction of the position line and a position through which it passes if star Capella had a sextant altitude of 60°14′.5 to an observer in D.R. position 30-45N, 072-12W when its G.H.A. was 104°58′. The observer's H.E. was 22 feet and the I.E. 2′.5 off the arc.

10. On August 26, 1968, at Z.T. = 0506 the star Aldebaran had a sextant altitude of 38°58′. If the chronometer was reading 17h58m42s at this time with an error of 6m48s slow of G.M.T., calculate the direction of the position line and a position through which it passes. The observer was in D.R. position 31-42S, 165-15E with H.E. 21 feet and I.E. 2′.8 on the arc.

39

FIXING POSITION

Using Celestial Position Lines

A single position line alone is insufficient to actually fix the vessel's position. Obviously further information, such as a second position line or a sounding, is required to isolate one spot on the first position line.

There are a number of different ways of using celestial position lines to obtain a fix. The most reliable and trusted method of obtaining a vessel's position by celestial observation is to use a number of star position lines taken simultaneously. However, as previously mentioned, star sights may only be taken when both the star and a reasonably clear horizon are visible. This confines star sights to a few minutes of twilight time during morning and evening. Bubble sextants with an artificial horizon have never proved effective at sea, mainly due to irregularities introduced by a ship's motion at sea. A typical illustration of simultaneous star sights is shown as follows.

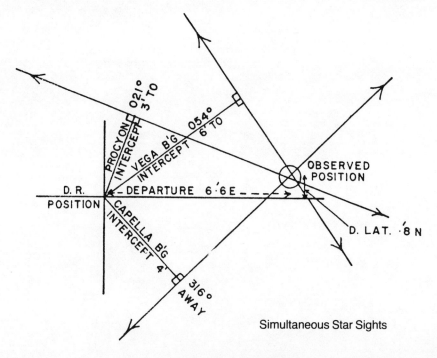

Simultaneous Star Sights

Star Identification

The approximate time of star sights can be extracted from the *Nautical Almanac*; it is usually about midway between sunrise or sunset and civil twilight. The approximate altitudes and azimuths of various stars may be precomputed so that the navigator can set the approximate altitude on his sextant and scan the horizon in the vicinity of the precomputed azimuth. This precomputing procedure is rather laborious and most navigators prefer to use some kind of star identifier. Probably the most popular device for star finding is No. 2102-D, produced by the United States Navy, and known to seamen the world over as the *Rude identifier*.

This star finder is very easy to use. The navigator simply selects one of the nine altitude azimuth plastic templates corresponding most nearly to his latitude and places this over the star base. Both templates and base have one side marked for the northern hemisphere and the other for the southern hemisphere. It is important to use the correct side. An arrow on the template is set to L.H.A. Aries on the star base, and the approximate altitudes and azimuths of the principal navigational stars can be read off.

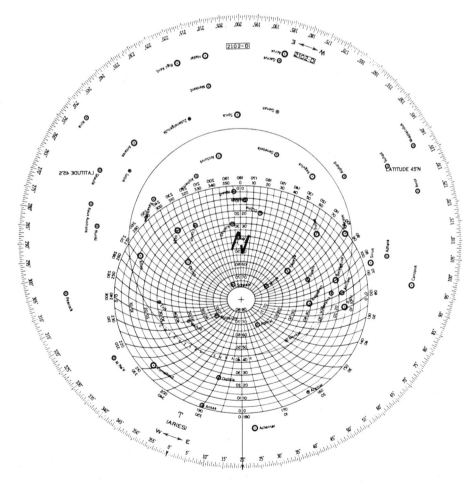

Star Identifier Set for Lat. 45°N, L.H.A. Aries 20°

Transferred Position Line

During the daylight hours, the navigator is dependent on the Sun for position lines. Occasionally planets can be observed during daylight hours if their altitude and azimuth are precomputed and they are searched for by sextant telescope. However, at this stage we will confine ourselves to obtaining separate position lines from observations of the Sun.

It is common practice to take morning sun sights when the Sun is at least 10° in altitude and as near east as possible. The resulting position line can then be transferred up to noon and crossed with the latitude position line obtained by meridian or exmeridian altitude in the same way as a running fix is determined for coastal chartwork.

Similarly, the Sun may be observed in the evening as near west as possible with an altitude of at least 10°. The position line can be transferred up to a latitude position line obtained by observation of the Pole Star.

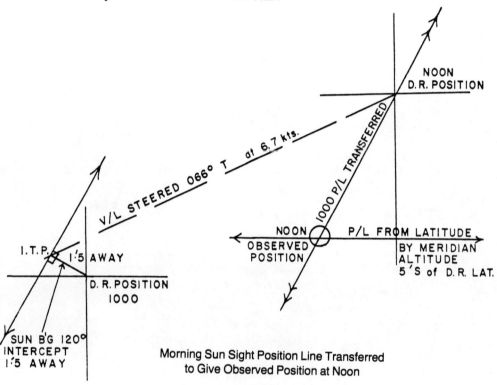

Morning Sun Sight Position Line Transferred
to Give Observed Position at Noon

Step 1.

The first position line is constructed from the D.R. position, and the I.T.P. is found by plotting or by using traverse tables.

Step 2.

The D.R. position at the time of the second observation is calculated by projecting the estimated course and speed made good away from the I.T.P. The first position line is transferred through this D.R. position.

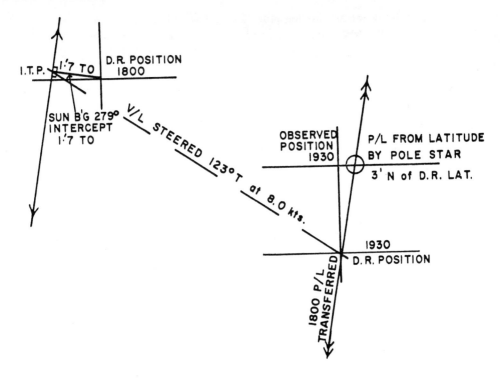

Evening Sun Sight Position Line Transferred
to Give Observed Position at Time
of Pole Star Observation

Step 3.

The intercept and azimuth, at the time of the new D.R. position, are laid off, and the new position line is constructed. Where the new position line intersects, the transferred position line is the observed position. The entire procedure can be carried out by plotting or can be done by calculation, using the traverse tables.

There are many different combinations of position lines, both transferred and instantaneous, terrestrial, and celestial, which can lead to a fix. When the basic principles of navigation are understood and practiced regularly, these more sophisticated thousands of miles out at sea. Celestial navigation will remain for a long time to come one of the finest arts practiced by seamen.

Exercise:
Fixing by Celestial Position Lines

1. A vessel in D.R. position 34-57N, 046-22W took simultaneous star sights of the following stars: Altair, bearing 242° T, intercept 1′ away; Vega, bearing 292° T, intercept 2.5′ away; and Fomalhaut, bearing 172° T, intercept 2′ towards. Calculate the vessel's observed position.

2. The following simultaneous star sights were observed by a vessel in D.R. position 36-22N, 068-13W: Deneb, bearing 060° T, intercept 2.5′ away; Altair, bearing 120° T, intercept .5′ towards; and Antares, bearing 195° T, intercept 3′ towards. Calculate the vessel's observed position.

3. At 0830 the Sun bearing 097° T gave an intercept of 4′ towards to a vessel in D.R. position 46-22N, 056-18W. The vessel steered 135° T at 10 knots until noon when the latitude by meridian altitude was 45-51N. State the observer's noon longitude.

4. In D.R. longitude 069-13W the latitude by meridian altitude of the Sun was 29-18N. The vessel ran 250° T at 11 knots from noon until 1700 when the Sun bearing 235° T gave an intercept of 8′ towards. Calculate the observer's position at 1700.

5. An observation of the Sun bearing 270° T gave an intercept of 3′ towards at 1730 hours in D.R. position 32-45N, 017-12W. The vessel then steered 050° T at 15 knots until 1930 hours when latitude by observation of the Pole Star was 33-08N. Calculate the observer's longitude at 1930 hours.

ANSWERS TO EXERCISES FOR PART II

Time

1. 0230
2. 1132
3. 02h16m48s
4. 23h10m17s
5. 13h02m20s

6. 12h54m31s
7. 21h38m06s
8. 09h08m09s
9. July 19, 2140
10. Dec. 21, 21h06m32s

Hour Angles

1. 138°14′
2. 37°36′
3. 31°19′
4. 339°04′
5. 044-36W

6. 020-54W
7. 15hr. 31 min.
8. 323°56′
9. 262°32′
10. 30°40′

Altitude Correction

1. 27°57′.9
2. 61°4′.3
3. 19°10′.3
4. 81°11′.9
5. 26°38′.5
6. 63°31′.8

7. 30°2′.8
8. 31°48′.8
9. 49°23′.7
10. 35°52′
    54°8′

Meridian Altitudes

1. 41-09S
2. 45-23S
3. 11-20N
4. 21½°S
5. 44-06.7N

6. 58-16.9N
7. 15-46.4N
8. 30-00.7N
9. 14h34m18s, 42-56.3S
10. 12h01m25s, 25-11.7N

Time Azimuths

1. 112.9° T
2. 162.1° T
3. 234.6° T
4. 300.0° T
5. 088.2° T

6. 14.5° E
7. 263.1° T
8. 25° W
9. 18.2° E
10. 1° E

Amplitudes

1. W 12° S
2. 063° T
3. W 31°N, 17° E

4. W
5. 14.7° W

Pole Star

1. 44-02N
2. 35-26N
3. 54-4.2N

4. 48-05.6N
5. 66-47.4N, 10° E

Sight Reduction

1. 014½°/194½°, 38-18.6N, 042-17.8W
   or 014°/194°, 37-56.5N, 042-24.7W
2. 121½°/301½°, 32-13.7N, 073-26.1W
   or 121°/301°, 32-13.8N, 073-26.2W
3. 001½°/181½°, 36-20.1N, 052-40.6W
   or 001.8°/181.8°, 36-00.5N, 52-41.0W
4. 015½°/195½°, 35-15.8N, 064-47W or
   015°/195°, 34-53.4N, 064-54.3W
5. 141.8°/321.8°, 31-03N, 125-08.5E or
   141.6°/321.6°, 31-10.8N, 125-01.2E

6. 032.2°/212.2°, 33-39N, 047-12.2W or
   032.6°/212.6°, 33-51.4N, 047-02.7W
7. 143.8°/323.8°, 33-07N, 048-05.6W or
   143.1°/323.1°, 33-07.2N, 048-05.6W
8. 170½°/350½°, 37-14.6N, 044-43W or
   170.3°/350.3°, 37-03N, 044-40.5W
9. 038°/218°, 30-50.6N, 071-43.9W or
   039.9°/219.9°, 30-50.2N, 071-44.3W
10. 112.2°/292.2°, 31-46S, 165-13.1E or
    112.3°/292.3°, 31-45.7S, 165-12.3E

Fixing by
Celestial Position Lines

1. 34-55.3N, 046-19.6W
2. 36-19.1N, 068-14.4W
3. 055-37W

4. 28-59.2N, 070-23.3W
5. 016-48W

APPENDIX: TABLE EXTRACTS

A2 ALTITUDE CORRECTION TABLES 10°–90°—SUN, STARS, PLANETS

OCT.–MAR. SUN APR.–SEPT.						STARS AND PLANETS				DIP			
App. Alt.	Lower Limb	Upper Limb	App. Alt.	Lower Limb	Upper Limb	App. Alt.	Corrⁿ	App. Alt.	Additional Corrⁿ	Ht. of Eye	Corrⁿ	Ht. of Eye	Corrⁿ
° ′			° ′			° ′	′			ft.		ft.	
9 34	+10·8	−22·7	9 39	+10·6	−22·4	9 56	−5·3	**1968**		1·1	−1·1	44	−6·5
9 45	+10·9	−22·6	9 51	+10·7	−22·3	10 08	−5·2			1·4	−1·2	45	−6·6
9 56	+11·0	−22·5	10 03	+10·8	−22·2	10 20	−5·1	**VENUS**		1·6	−1·3	47	−6·7
10 08	+11·1	−22·4	10 15	+10·9	−22·1	10 33	−5·0			1·9	−1·4	48	−6·8
10 21	+11·2	−22·3	10 27	+11·0	−22·0	10 46	−4·9	Jan. 1–Dec. 14		2·2	−1·5	49	−6·9
10 34	+11·3	−22·2	10 40	+11·1	−21·9	11 00	−4·8			2·5	−1·6	51	−7·0
10 47	+11·4	−22·1	10 54	+11·2	−21·8	11 14	−4·7	0″	+0·1	2·8	−1·7	52	−7·1
11 01	+11·5	−22·0	11 08	+11·3	−21·7	11 29	−4·6	42		3·2	−1·8	54	−7·2
11 15	+11·6	−21·9	11 23	+11·4	−21·6	11 45	−4·5			3·6	−1·9	55	−7·3
11 30	+11·7	−21·8	11 38	+11·5	−21·5	12 01	−4·4	Dec. 15–Dec. 31		4·0	−2·0	57	−7·4
11 46	+11·8	−21·7	11 54	+11·6	−21·4	12 18	−4·3			4·4	−2·1	58	−7·5
12 02	+11·9	−21·6	12 10	+11·7	−21·3	12 35	−4·2	0″	+0·2	4·9	−2·2	60	−7·6
12 19	+12·0	−21·5	12 28	+11·8	−21·2	12 54	−4·1	47		5·3	−2·3	62	−7·7
12 37	+12·1	−21·4	12 46	+11·9	−21·1	13 13	−4·0			5·8	−2·4	63	−7·8
12 55	+12·2	−21·3	13 05	+12·0	−21·0	13 33	−3·9			6·3	−2·5	65	−7·9
13 14	+12·3	−21·2	13 24	+12·1	−20·9	13 54	−3·8			6·9	−2·6	67	−8·0
13 35	+12·4	−21·1	13 45	+12·2	−20·8	14 16	−3·7			7·4	−2·7	68	−8·1
13 56	+12·5	−21·0	14 07	+12·3	−20·7	14 40	−3·6			8·0	−2·8	70	−8·2
14 18	+12·6	−20·9	14 30	+12·4	−20·6	15 04	−3·5			8·6	−2·9	72	−8·3
14 42	+12·7	−20·8	14 54	+12·5	−20·5	15 30	−3·4			9·2	−3·0	74	−8·4
15 06	+12·8	−20·7	15 19	+12·6	−20·4	15 57	−3·3			9·8	−3·1	75	−8·5
15 32	+12·9	−20·6	15 46	+12·7	−20·3	16 26	−3·2			10·5	−3·2	77	−8·6
15 59	+13·0	−20·5	16 14	+12·8	−20·2	16 56	−3·1			11·2	−3·3	79	−8·7
16 28	+13·1	−20·4	16 44	+12·9	−20·1	17 28	−3·0			11·9	−3·4	81	−8·8
16 59	+13·2	−20·3	17 15	+13·0	−20·0	18 02	−2·9			12·6	−3·5	83	−8·9
17 32	+13·3	−20·2	17 48	+13·1	−19·9	18 38	−2·8			13·3	−3·6	85	−9·0
18 06	+13·4	−20·1	18 24	+13·2	−19·8	19 17	−2·7	**MARS**		14·1	−3·7	87	−9·1
18 42	+13·5	−20·0	19 01	+13·3	−19·7	19 58	−2·6	Jan. 1–Dec. 31		14·9	−3·8	88	−9·2
19 21	+13·6	−19·9	19 42	+13·4	−19·6	20 42	−2·5			15·7	−3·9	90	−9·3
20 03	+13·7	−19·8	20 25	+13·5	−19·5	21 28	−2·4	0″	+0·1	16·5	−4·0	92	−9·4
20 48	+13·8	−19·7	21 11	+13·6	−19·4	22 19	−2·3	60		17·4	−4·1	94	−9·5
21 35	+13·9	−19·6	22 00	+13·7	−19·3	23 13	−2·2			18·3	−4·2	96	−9·6
22 26	+14·0	−19·5	22 54	+13·8	−19·2	24 11	−2·1			19·1	−4·3	98	−9·7
23 22	+14·1	−19·4	23 51	+13·9	−19·1	25 14	−2·0			20·1	−4·4	101	−9·8
24 21	+14·2	−19·3	24 53	+14·0	−19·0	26 22	−1·9			21·0	−4·5	103	−9·9
25 26	+14·3	−19·2	26 00	+14·1	−18·9	27 36	−1·8			22·0	−4·6	105	−10·0
26 36	+14·4	−19·1	27 13	+14·2	−18·8	28 56	−1·7			22·9	−4·7	107	−10·1
27 52	+14·5	−19·0	28 33	+14·3	−18·7	30 24	−1·6			23·9	−4·8	109	−10·2
29 15	+14·6	−18·9	30 00	+14·4	−18·6	32 00	−1·5			24·9	−4·9	111	−10·3
30 46	+14·7	−18·8	31 35	+14·5	−18·5	33 45	−1·4			26·0	−5·0	113	−10·4
32 26	+14·8	−18·7	33 20	+14·6	−18·4	35 40	−1·3			27·1	−5·1	116	−10·5
34 17	+14·9	−18·6	35 17	+14·7	−18·3	37 48	−1·2			28·1	−5·2	118	−10·6
36 20	+15·0	−18·5	37 26	+14·8	−18·2	40 08	−1·1			29·2	−5·3	120	−10·7
38 36	+15·1	−18·4	39 50	+14·9	−18·1	42 44	−1·0			30·4	−5·4	122	−10·8
41 08	+15·2	−18·3	42 31	+15·0	−18·0	45 36	−0·9			31·5	−5·5	125	−10·9
43 59	+15·3	−18·2	45 31	+15·1	−17·9	48 47	−0·8			32·7	−5·6	127	−11·0
47 10	+15·4	−18·1	48 55	+15·2	−17·8	52 18	−0·7			33·9	−5·7	129	−11·1
50 46	+15·5	−18·0	52 44	+15·3	−17·7	56 11	−0·6			35·1	−5·8	132	−11·2
54 49	+15·6	−17·9	57 02	+15·4	−17·6	60 28	−0·5			36·3	−5·9	134	−11·3
59 23	+15·7	−17·8	61 51	+15·5	−17·5	65 08	−0·4			37·6	−6·0	136	−11·4
64 30	+15·8	−17·7	67 17	+15·6	−17·4	70 11	−0·3			38·9	−6·1	139	−11·5
70 12	+15·9	−17·6	73 16	+15·7	−17·3	75 34	−0·2			40·1	−6·2	141	−11·6
76 26	+16·0	−17·5	79 43	+15·8	−17·2	81 13	−0·1			41·5	−6·3	144	−11·7
83 05	+16·1	−17·4	86 32	+15·9	−17·1	87 03	0·0			42·8	−6·4	146	−11·8
90 00			90 00			90 00				44·2		149	

App. Alt. = Apparent altitude = Sextant altitude corrected for index error and dip.

For daylight observations of Venus, see page 260.

POLARIS (POLE STAR) TABLES, 1968   275
FOR DETERMINING LATITUDE FROM SEXTANT ALTITUDE AND FOR AZIMUTH

L.H.A. ARIES	120°–129°	130°–139°	140°–149°	150°–159°	160°–169°	170°–179°	180°–189°	190°–199°	200°–209°	210°–219°	220°–229°	230°–239°
	a_0	a_0	a_0	a_0	a_0	a_0	a_0	a_0	a_0	a_0	a_0	a_0
0	0 59·0	1 08·1	1 17·0	1 25·2	1 32·7	1 39·2	1 44·4	1 48·3	1 50·7	1 51·5	1 50·8	1 48·5
1	0 59·9	09·0	17·8	26·0	33·4	39·7	44·9	48·6	50·8	51·5	50·6	48·2
2	1 00·8	09·9	18·7	26·8	34·1	40·3	45·3	48·9	51·0	51·5	50·4	47·8
3	01·7	10·8	19·5	27·6	34·8	40·9	45·7	49·2	51·1	51·4	50·2	47·5
4	02·7	11·7	20·4	28·3	35·4	41·4	46·1	49·4	51·2	51·4	50·0	47·1
5	1 03·6	1 12·6	1 21·2	1 29·1	1 36·1	1 41·9	1 46·5	1 49·7	1 51·3	1 51·3	1 49·8	1 46·8
6	04·5	13·5	22·0	29·8	36·7	42·5	46·9	49·9	51·4	51·2	49·6	46·4
7	05·4	14·4	22·8	30·6	37·3	43·0	47·3	50·1	51·4	51·1	49·3	46·0
8	06·3	15·2	23·6	31·3	38·0	43·5	47·6	50·3	51·5	51·0	49·1	45·6
9	07·2	16·1	24·4	32·0	38·6	43·9	48·0	50·5	51·5	50·9	48·8	45·2
10	1 08·1	1 17·0	1 25·2	1 32·7	1 39·2	1 44·4	1 48·3	1 50·7	1 51·5	1 50·8	1 48·5	1 44·7

Lat.	a_1	a_1	a_1	a_1	a_1	a_1	a_1	a_1	a_1	a_1	a_1	a_1
0	0·1	0·2	0·2	0·3	0·4	0·4	0·5	0·6	0·6	0·6	0·6	0·5
10	·2	·2	·3	·3	·4	·5	·5	·6	·6	·6	·6	·5
20	·3	·3	·3	·4	·4	·5	·5	·6	·6	·6	·6	·5
30	·4	·4	·4	·4	·5	·5	·6	·6	·6	·6	·6	·6
40	0·5	0·5	0·5	0·5	0·5	0·6	0·6	0·6	0·6	0·6	0·6	0·6
45	·5	·5	·5	·5	·6	·6	·6	·6	·6	·6	·6	·6
50	·6	·6	·6	·6	·6	·6	·6	·6	·6	·6	·6	·6
55	·7	·7	·7	·7	·6	·6	·6	·6	·6	·6	·6	·6
60	·8	·8	·8	·7	·7	·7	·6	·6	·6	·6	·6	·6
62	0·9	0·9	0·8	0·8	0·7	0·7	0·7	0·6	0·6	0·6	0·6	0·6
64	0·9	0·9	0·9	·8	·8	·7	·7	·6	·6	·6	·6	·7
66	1·0	1·0	1·0	0·9	·8	·7	·7	·6	·6	·6	·6	·7
68	1·1	1·1	1·0	1·0	0·9	0·8	0·7	0·6	0·6	0·6	0·6	0·7

Month	a_2	a_2	a_2	a_2	a_2	a_2	a_2	a_2	a_2	a_2	a_2	a_2
Jan.	0·6	0·6	0·6	0·6	0·6	0·5	0·5	0·5	0·5	0·5	0·5	0·5
Feb.	·8	·7	·7	·7	·7	·6	·6	·6	·6	·5	·5	·5
Mar.	·9	·9	0·9	0·8	·8	·8	·8	·7	·7	·6	·6	·5
Apr.	0·9	0·9	1·0	1·0	0·9	0·9	0·9	0·9	0·8	0·7	0·7	0·6
May	·9	·9	1·0	1·0	1·0	1·0	1·0	1·0	0·9	0·9	·8	·8
June	·8	·8	0·9	0·9	1·0	1·0	1·0	1·0	1·0	1·0	0·9	0·9
July	0·6	0·7	0·8	0·8	0·9	0·9	1·0	1·0	1·0	1·0	1·0	1·0
Aug.	·4	·5	·6	·6	·7	·8	0·8	0·9	0·9	1·0	1·0	1·0
Sept.	·3	·4	·4	·5	·5	·6	·7	·7	·8	0·8	0·9	0·9
Oct.	0·2	0·2	0·3	0·3	0·3	0·4	0·5	0·5	0·6	0·7	0·7	0·8
Nov.	·2	·2	·2	·2	·2	·3	·3	·3	·4	·5	·5	·6
Dec.	0·3	0·2	0·2	0·2	0·2	0·2	0·2	0·2	0·3	0·3	0·4	0·5

Lat.	AZIMUTH											
0	359·1	359·2	359·2	359·3	359·4	359·5	359·6	359·8	359·9	0·1	0·2	0·4
20	359·1	359·1	359·1	359·2	359·3	359·5	359·6	359·7	359·9	0·1	0·2	0·4
40	358·9	358·9	359·0	359·1	359·2	359·3	359·5	359·7	359·9	0·1	0·3	0·5
50	358·6	358·7	358·8	358·9	359·0	359·2	359·4	359·6	359·9	0·1	0·3	0·6
55	358·5	358·5	358·6	358·8	358·9	359·1	359·4	359·6	359·9	0·1	0·4	0·6
60	358·2	358·3	358·4	358·6	358·8	359·0	359·3	359·5	359·8	0·1	0·4	0·7
65	357·9	358·0	358·1	358·3	358·6	358·8	359·1	359·5	359·8	0·2	0·5	0·8

ILLUSTRATION

On 1968 January 22 at G.M.T. 22ʰ 17ᵐ 50ˢ in longitude W. 55° 19′ the corrected apparent altitude of *Polaris* was 49° 31′·6.

From the daily pages :	° ′
G.H.A. Aries (22ʰ)	91 19·3
Increment (17ᵐ 50ˢ)	4 28·2
Longitude (west)	−55 19
L.H.A. Aries	40 29

	° ′
Corr. App. Alt.	49 31·6
a_0 (argument 40° 29′)	0 06·9
a_1 (lat. 50° approx.)	0·6
a_2 (January)	0·7
Sum − 1° = Lat. =	48 39·8

1968 AUGUST 25, 26, 27 (SUN., MON., TUES.)

G.M.T.	ARIES G.H.A.	VENUS −3.3 G.H.A.	Dec.	MARS +2.0 G.H.A.	Dec.	JUPITER −1.2 G.H.A.	Dec.	SATURN +0.5 G.H.A.	Dec.	STARS Name	S.H.A.	Dec.
d h	° ′	° ′	° ′	° ′	° ′	° ′	° ′	° ′	° ′		° ′	° ′
25 00	333 19·1	162 09·5 N 5 15·4		198 07·2 N18 09·8		168 28·0 N 7 33·0		308 54·9 N 7 17·9		Acamar	315 43·7	S 40 25·4
01	348 21·6	177 09·1	14·2	213 08·0	09·3	183 29·9	32·8	323 57·4	17·8	Achernar	335 51·2	S 57 23·4
02	3 24·1	192 08·8	12·9	228 08·9	08·9	198 31·9	32·6	339 00·0	17·8	Acrux	173 48·2	S 62 55·6
03	18 26·5	207 08·4 ·· 11·7		243 09·7 ·· 08·4		213 33·9 ·· 32·4		354 02·5 ·· 17·8		Adhara	255 39·4	S 28 55·3
04	33 29·0	222 08·0	10·4	258 10·6	08·0	228 35·8	32·2	9 05·0	17·7	Aldebaran	291 28·3	N 16 27·0
05	48 31·5	237 07·7	09·1	273 11·4	07·6	243 37·8	32·0	24 07·6	17·7			
06	63 33·9	252 07·3 N 5 07·9		288 12·3 N18 07·1		258 39·8 N 7 31·8		39 10·1 N 7 17·6		Alioth	166 50·4	N 56 08·0
07	78 36·4	267 07·0	06·6	303 13·1	06·7	273 41·7	31·6	54 12·6	17·6	Alkaid	153 25·5	N 49 28·4
08	93 38·9	282 06·6	05·4	318 14·0	06·2	288 43·7	31·4	69 15·2	17·6	Al Na'ir	28 25·5	S 47 06·8
S 09	108 41·3	297 06·2 ·· 04·1		333 14·8 ·· 05·8		303 45·7 ·· 31·2		84 17·7 ·· 17·5		Alnilam	276 20·9	S 1 13·0
U 10	123 43·8	312 05·9	02·9	348 15·7	05·3	318 47·6	31·0	99 20·2	17·5	Alphard	218 29·7	S 8 31·1
N 11	138 46·3	327 05·5	01·6	3 16·5	04·9	333 49·6	30·8	114 22·8	17·5			
D 12	153 48·7	342 05·2 N 5 00·4		18 17·4 N18 04·5		348 51·5 N 7 30·6		129 25·3 N 7 17·4		Alphecca	126 39·7	N 26 49·3
A 13	168 51·2	357 04·8 4 59·1		33 18·2	04·0	3 53·5	30·4	144 27·8	17·4	Alpheratz	358 18·4	N 28 55·1
Y 14	183 53·6	12 04·5	57·9	48 19·1	03·6	18 55·5	30·2	159 30·4	17·3	Altair	62 41·0	N 8 47·1
15	198 56·1	27 04·1 ·· 56·6		63 19·9 ·· 03·1		33 57·4 ·· 30·0		174 32·9 ·· 17·3		Ankaa	353 48·5	S 42 28·3
16	213 58·6	42 03·7	55·4	78 20·8	02·7	48 59·4	29·8	189 35·4	17·3	Antares	113 07·8	S 26 22·0
17	229 01·0	57 03·4	54·1	93 21·6	02·2	64 01·4	29·6	204 38·0	17·2			
18	244 03·5	72 03·0 N 4 52·9		108 22·5 N18 01·8		79 03·3 N 7 29·4		219 40·5 N 7 17·2		Arcturus	146 26·7	N 19 20·8
19	259 06·0	87 02·7	51·6	123 23·3	01·4	94 05·3	29·1	234 43·0	17·2	Atria	108 40·1	S 68 58·7
20	274 08·4	102 02·3	50·3	138 24·2	00·9	109 07·3	28·9	249 45·6	17·1	Avior	234 32·6	S 59 24·2
21	289 10·9	117 02·0 ·· 49·1		153 25·0 ·· 00·5		124 09·2 ·· 28·7		264 48·1 ·· 17·1		Bellatrix	279 08·4	N 6 19·6
22	304 13·4	132 01·6	47·8	168 25·9 18 00·0		139 11·2	28·5	279 50·6	17·0	Betelgeuse	271 38·1	N 7 24·4
23	319 15·8	147 01·2	46·6	183 26·7 17 59·6		154 13·2	28·3	294 53·2	17·0			
26 00	334 18·3	162 00·9 N 4 45·3		198 27·6 N17 59·1		169 15·1 N 7 28·1		309 55·7 N 7 17·0		Canopus	264 11·5	S 52 40·2
01	349 20·7	177 00·5	44·1	213 28·4	58·7	184 17·1	27·9	324 58·2	16·9	Capella	281 24·6	N 45 58·1
02	4 23·2	192 00·2	42·8	228 29·3	58·2	199 19·1	27·7	340 00·8	16·9	Deneb	49 54·3	N 45 10·1
03	19 25·7	206 59·8 ·· 41·6		243 30·2 ·· 57·8		214 21·0 ·· 27·5		355 03·3 ·· 16·8		Denebola	183 08·4	N 14 45·0
04	34 28·1	221 59·5	40·3	258 31·0	57·4	229 23·0	27·3	10 05·9	16·8	Diphda	349 29·5	S 18 09·3
05	49 30·6	236 59·1	39·0	273 31·9	56·9	244 24·9	27·1	25 08·4	16·8			
06	64 33·1	251 58·8 N 4 37·8		288 32·7 N17 56·5		259 26·9 N 7 26·9		40 10·9 N 7 16·7		Dubhe	194 33·3	N 61 55·4
07	79 35·5	266 58·4	36·5	303 33·6	56·0	274 28·9	26·7	55 13·5	16·7	Elnath	278 55·6	N 28 35·1
08	94 38·0	281 58·1	35·3	318 34·4	55·6	289 30·8	26·5	70 16·0	16·7	Eltanin	91 01·6	N 51 29·7
M 09	109 40·5	296 57·7 ·· 34·0		333 35·3 ·· 55·1		304 32·8 ·· 26·3		85 18·5 ·· 16·6		Enif	34 20·1	N 9 43·9
O 10	124 42·9	311 57·4	32·7	348 36·1	54·7	319 34·8	26·1	100 21·1	16·6	Fomalhaut	16 00·8	S 29 47·2
N 11	139 45·4	326 57·0	31·5	3 37·0	54·2	334 36·7	25·9	115 23·6	16·5			
D 12	154 47·8	341 56·6 N 4 30·2		18 37·8 N17 53·8		349 38·7 N 7 25·6		130 26·2 N 7 16·5		Gacrux	172 39·5	S 56 56·4
A 13	169 50·3	356 56·3	29·0	33 38·7	53·3	4 40·7	25·4	145 28·7	16·5	Gienah	176 27·5	S 17 22·0
Y 14	184 52·8	11 55·9	27·7	48 39·5	52·9	19 42·6	25·2	160 31·2	16·4	Hadar	149 36·7	S 60 13·6
15	199 55·2	26 55·6 ·· 26·5		63 40·4 ·· 52·4		34 44·6 ·· 25·0		175 33·8 ·· 16·4		Hamal	328 38·9	N 23 19·0
16	214 57·7	41 55·2	25·2	78 41·3	52·0	49 46·5	24·8	190 36·3	16·3	Kaus Aust.	84 28·4	S 34 24·3
17	230 00·2	56 54·9	23·9	93 42·1	51·5	64 48·5	24·6	205 38·8	16·3			
18	245 02·6	71 54·5 N 4 22·7		108 43·0 N17 51·1		79 50·5 N 7 24·4		220 41·4 N 7 16·3		Kochab	137 18·3	N 74 17·2
19	260 05·1	86 54·2	21·4	123 43·8	50·6	94 52·4	24·2	235 43·9	16·2	Markab	14 11·8	N 15 02·2
20	275 07·6	101 53·8	20·2	138 44·7	50·2	109 54·4	24·0	250 46·5	16·2	Menkar	314 50·4	N 3 58·3
21	290 10·0	116 53·5 ·· 18·9		153 45·5 ·· 49·7		124 56·4 ·· 23·8		265 49·0 ·· 16·1		Menkent	148 47·9	S 36 13·1
22	305 12·5	131 53·1	17·6	168 46·4	49·3	139 58·3	23·6	280 51·5	16·1	Miaplacidus	221 48·2	S 69 35·0
23	320 15·0	146 52·8	16·4	183 47·2	48·9	155 00·3	23·4	295 54·1	16·1			
27 00	335 17·4	161 52·4 N 4 15·1		198 48·1 N17 48·4		170 02·3 N 7 23·2		310 56·6 N 7 16·0		Mirfak	309 29·0	N 49 45·0
01	350 19·9	176 52·1	13·8	213 49·0	48·0	185 04·2	23·0	325 59·2	16·0	Nunki	76 40·0	S 26 20·4
02	5 22·3	191 51·7	12·6	228 49·8	47·5	200 06·2	22·8	341 01·7	15·9	Peacock	54 11·7	S 56 50·4
03	20 24·8	206 51·4 ·· 11·3		243 50·7 ·· 47·1		215 08·1 ·· 22·6		356 04·2 ·· 15·9		Pollux	244 09·3	N 28 06·4
04	35 27·3	221 51·0	10·1	258 51·5	46·6	230 10·1	22·3	11 06·8	15·9	Procyon	245 35·3	N 5 18·6
05	50 29·7	236 50·7	08·8	273 52·4	46·2	245 12·1	22·1	26 09·3	15·8			
06	65 32·2	251 50·3 N 4 07·5		288 53·2 N17 45·7		260 14·0 N 7 21·9		41 11·9 N 7 15·8		Rasalhague	96 37·7	N 12 34·9
07	80 34·7	266 50·0	06·3	303 54·1	45·2	275 16·0	21·7	56 14·4	15·7	Regulus	208 19·8	N 12 07·5
T 08	95 37·1	281 49·6	05·0	318 55·0	44·8	290 18·0	21·5	71 16·9	15·7	Rigel	281 44·7	S 8 13·9
U 09	110 39·6	296 49·3 ·· 03·7		333 55·8 ·· 44·3		305 19·9 ·· 21·3		86 19·5 ·· 15·7		Rigil Kent.	140 38·5	S 60 42·6
E 10	125 42·1	311 48·9	02·5	348 56·7	43·9	320 21·9	21·1	101 22·0	15·6	Sabik	102 51·3	S 15 41·4
S 11	140 44·5	326 48·6	4 01·2	3 57·5	43·4	335 23·9	20·9	116 24·6	15·6			
D 12	155 47·0	341 48·2 N 3 59·9		18 58·4 N17 43·0		350 25·8 N 7 20·7		131 27·1 N 7 15·5		Schedar	350 19·1	N 56 21·9
A 13	170 49·4	356 47·9	58·7	33 59·2	42·5	5 27·8	20·5	146 29·6	15·5	Shaula	97 07·8	S 37 05·2
Y 14	185 51·9	11 47·6	57·4	49 00·1	42·1	20 29·7	20·3	161 32·2	15·5	Sirius	259 03·8	S 16 40·0
15	200 54·4	26 47·2 ·· 56·2		64 01·0 ·· 41·6		35 31·7 ·· 20·1		176 34·7 ·· 15·4		Spica	159 07·2	S 10 59·8
16	215 56·8	41 46·9	54·9	79 01·8	41·2	50 33·7	19·9	191 37·3	15·4	Suhail	223 17·9	S 43 18·1
17	230 59·3	56 46·5	53·6	94 02·7	40·7	65 35·6	19·7	206 39·8	15·3			
18	246 01·8	71 46·2 N 3 52·4		109 03·5 N17 40·3		80 37·6 N 7 19·5		221 42·4 N 7 15·3		Vega	81 01·7	N 38 45·3
19	261 04·2	86 45·8	51·1	124 04·4	39·8	95 39·6	19·3	236 44·9	15·3	Zuben'ubi	137 43·1	S 15 54·8
20	276 06·7	101 45·5	49·8	139 05·3	39·4	110 41·5	19·0	251 47·4	15·2			
21	291 09·2	116 45·1 ·· 48·6		154 06·1 ·· 38·9		125 43·5 ·· 18·8		266 50·0 ·· 15·2			S.H.A.	Mer. Pass.
22	306 11·6	131 44·8	47·3	169 07·0	38·5	140 45·5	18·6	281 52·5	15·1		° ′	h m
23	321 14·1	146 44·4	46·0	184 07·8	38·0	155 47·4	18·4	296 55·1	15·1	Venus	187 42·6	13 12
										Mars	224 09·3	10 46
Mer. Pass.	1 42·5	v −0·4 d 1·3		v 0·9 d 0·4		v 2·0 d 0·2		v 2·5 d 0·0		Jupiter	194 56·8	12 41
										Saturn	335 37·4	3 20

1968 AUGUST 25, 26, 27 (SUN., MON., TUES.)

G.M.T.	SUN G.H.A.	SUN Dec.	MOON G.H.A.	v	MOON Dec.	d	H.P.
25 00	179 28.2	N10 49.2	166 55.3	13.2	N 8 16.0	15.6	57.7
01	194 28.3	48.4	181 27.5	13.2	8 00.4	15.6	57.7
02	209 28.5	47.5	195 59.7	13.2	7 44.8	15.7	57.7
03	224 28.7	.. 46.7	210 31.9	13.2	7 29.1	15.8	57.8
04	239 28.8	45.8	225 04.1	13.2	7 13.3	15.7	57.8
05	254 29.0	44.9	239 36.3	13.3	6 57.6	15.8	57.8
06	269 29.2	N10 44.1	254 08.6	13.2	N 6 41.8	15.9	57.8
07	284 29.4	43.2	268 40.8	13.3	6 25.9	15.9	57.8
08	299 29.5	42.3	283 13.1	13.2	6 10.0	16.0	57.9
S 09	314 29.7	.. 41.5	297 45.3	13.3	5 54.0	15.9	57.9
U 10	329 29.9	40.6	312 17.6	13.3	5 38.1	16.0	57.9
N 11	344 30.0	39.7	326 49.9	13.3	5 22.1	16.1	57.9
D 12	359 30.2	N10 38.9	341 22.2	13.3	N 5 06.0	16.1	57.9
A 13	14 30.4	38.0	355 54.5	13.3	4 49.9	16.1	58.0
Y 14	29 30.6	37.1	10 26.8	13.3	4 33.8	16.2	58.0
15	44 30.7	.. 36.3	24 59.1	13.3	4 17.6	16.1	58.0
16	59 30.9	35.4	39 31.4	13.3	4 01.5	16.2	58.0
17	74 31.1	34.5	54 03.7	13.3	3 45.3	16.3	58.0
18	89 31.3	N10 33.7	68 36.0	13.3	N 3 29.0	16.2	58.1
19	104 31.4	32.8	83 08.3	13.4	3 12.8	16.3	58.1
20	119 31.6	31.9	97 40.7	13.3	2 56.5	16.4	58.1
21	134 31.8	.. 31.1	112 13.0	13.2	2 40.1	16.3	58.1
22	149 31.9	30.2	126 45.2	13.3	2 23.8	16.3	58.1
23	164 32.1	29.3	141 17.5	13.3	2 07.5	16.4	58.2
26 00	179 32.3	N10 28.5	155 49.8	13.3	N 1 51.1	16.4	58.2
01	194 32.5	27.6	170 22.1	13.3	1 34.7	16.4	58.2
02	209 32.6	26.7	184 54.4	13.2	1 18.3	16.5	58.2
03	224 32.8	.. 25.9	199 26.6	13.2	1 01.8	16.4	58.2
04	239 33.0	25.0	213 58.9	13.2	0 45.4	16.5	58.2
05	254 33.2	24.1	228 31.1	13.2	0 28.9	16.4	58.3
06	269 33.3	N10 23.3	243 03.3	13.2	N 0 12.5	16.5	58.3
07	284 33.5	22.4	257 35.5	13.2	S 0 04.0	16.5	58.3
08	299 33.7	21.5	272 07.7	13.1	0 20.5	16.5	58.3
M 09	314 33.9	.. 20.6	286 39.8	13.2	0 37.0	16.5	58.3
O 10	329 34.0	19.8	301 12.0	13.1	0 53.5	16.5	58.4
N 11	344 34.2	18.9	315 44.1	13.1	1 10.0	16.5	58.4
D 12	359 34.4	N10 18.0	330 16.2	13.1	S 1 26.5	16.5	58.4
A 13	14 34.6	17.2	344 48.3	13.1	1 43.0	16.5	58.4
Y 14	29 34.7	16.3	359 20.4	13.0	1 59.5	16.5	58.4
15	44 34.9	.. 15.4	13 52.4	13.0	2 16.0	16.5	58.4
16	59 35.1	14.5	28 24.4	13.0	2 32.5	16.5	58.5
17	74 35.3	13.7	42 56.4	12.9	2 49.0	16.5	58.5
18	89 35.5	N10 12.8	57 28.3	12.9	S 3 05.5	16.5	58.5
19	104 35.6	11.9	72 00.2	12.9	3 22.0	16.5	58.5
20	119 35.8	11.0	86 32.1	12.9	3 38.5	16.5	58.5
21	134 36.0	.. 10.2	101 04.0	12.8	3 55.0	16.5	58.5
22	149 36.2	09.3	115 35.8	12.8	4 11.5	16.4	58.6
23	164 36.3	08.4	130 07.6	12.7	4 27.9	16.6	58.6
27 00	179 36.5	N10 07.5	144 39.3	12.7	S 4 44.3	16.5	58.6
01	194 36.7	06.7	159 11.0	12.7	5 00.8	16.4	58.6
02	209 36.9	05.8	173 42.7	12.6	5 17.2	16.4	58.6
03	224 37.0	.. 04.9	188 14.3	12.6	5 33.6	16.3	58.6
04	239 37.2	04.0	202 45.9	12.6	5 49.9	16.4	58.6
05	254 37.4	03.2	217 17.5	12.5	6 06.3	16.3	58.7
06	269 37.6	N10 02.3	231 49.0	12.4	S 6 22.6	16.3	58.7
07	284 37.8	01.4	246 20.4	12.4	6 38.9	16.3	58.7
T 08	299 37.9	10 00.5	260 51.8	12.4	6 55.2	16.2	58.7
U 09	314 38.1	9 59.6	275 23.2	12.3	7 11.4	16.2	58.7
E 10	329 38.3	58.8	289 54.5	12.3	7 27.6	16.2	58.7
S 11	344 38.5	57.9	304 25.8	12.2	7 43.8	16.2	58.7
D 12	359 38.7	N 9 57.0	318 57.0	12.1	S 8 00.0	16.1	58.8
A 13	14 38.8	56.1	333 28.1	12.1	8 16.1	16.1	58.8
Y 14	29 39.0	55.2	347 59.2	12.1	8 32.2	16.1	58.8
15	44 39.2	.. 54.4	2 30.3	12.0	8 48.3	16.0	58.8
16	59 39.4	53.5	17 01.3	11.9	9 04.3	16.0	58.8
17	74 39.6	52.6	31 32.2	11.9	9 20.3	15.9	58.8
18	89 39.8	N 9 51.7	46 03.1	11.8	S 9 36.2	15.9	58.8
19	104 39.9	50.8	60 33.9	11.8	9 52.1	15.8	58.8
20	119 40.1	50.0	75 04.7	11.7	10 07.9	15.8	58.9
21	134 40.3	.. 49.1	89 35.4	11.6	10 23.7	15.8	58.9
22	149 40.5	48.2	104 06.0	11.5	10 39.5	15.7	58.9
23	164 40.7	47.3	118 36.5	11.5	10 55.2	15.7	58.9
	S.D. 15.9	d 0.9	S.D. 15.8		15.9		16.0

Lat.	Twilight Naut.	Twilight Civil	Sun-rise	Moonrise 25	Moonrise 26	Moonrise 27	Moonrise 28
N 72	////	01 39	03 30	05 39	07 57	10 19	13 09
N 70	////	02 23	03 49	05 49	07 57	10 07	12 34
68	////	02 51	04 03	05 57	07 56	09 57	12 10
66	01 25	03 12	04 15	06 04	07 56	09 49	11 52
64	02 04	03 29	04 25	06 10	07 55	09 43	11 37
62	02 31	03 42	04 33	06 15	07 55	09 37	11 24
60	02 50	03 54	04 40	06 19	07 55	09 32	11 14
N 58	03 06	04 03	04 47	06 22	07 54	09 28	11 05
56	03 19	04 12	04 52	06 26	07 54	09 24	10 57
54	03 31	04 19	04 57	06 29	07 54	09 21	10 50
52	03 40	04 26	05 02	06 31	07 54	09 18	10 44
50	03 49	04 31	05 06	06 34	07 54	09 15	10 38
45	04 06	04 44	05 15	06 39	07 53	09 09	10 25
N 40	04 20	04 54	05 22	06 44	07 53	09 04	10 16
35	04 31	05 02	05 28	06 47	07 53	08 59	10 08
30	04 40	05 09	05 34	06 51	07 53	08 56	10 01
20	04 54	05 20	05 43	06 56	07 52	08 49	09 48
N 10	05 05	05 30	05 51	07 01	07 52	08 44	09 37
0	05 13	05 37	05 58	07 06	07 52	08 38	09 27
S 10	05 20	05 45	06 06	07 11	07 52	08 33	09 17
20	05 25	05 51	06 13	07 16	07 51	08 28	09 06
30	05 30	05 58	06 22	07 21	07 51	08 22	08 54
35	05 32	06 02	06 27	07 24	07 51	08 18	08 47
40	05 34	06 05	06 33	07 28	07 51	08 14	08 39
45	05 35	06 09	06 39	07 32	07 51	08 10	08 30
S 50	05 37	06 14	06 47	07 37	07 51	08 04	08 20
52	05 37	06 16	06 50	07 40	07 51	08 02	08 15
54	05 37	06 18	06 54	07 42	07 51	07 59	08 09
56	05 38	06 21	06 59	07 45	07 50	07 56	08 03
58	05 38	06 23	07 03	07 48	07 50	07 53	07 56
S 60	05 38	06 26	07 09	07 51	07 50	07 49	07 49

Lat.	Sun-set	Twilight Civil	Twilight Naut.	Moonset 25	Moonset 26	Moonset 27	Moonset 28
N 72	20 29	22 16	////	20 04	19 28	18 46	17 41
N 70	20 12	21 36	////	20 00	19 32	19 02	18 18
68	19 57	21 08	////	19 57	19 36	19 14	18 44
66	19 46	20 48	22 30	19 54	19 40	19 24	19 04
64	19 37	20 32	21 54	19 52	19 43	19 32	19 20
62	19 29	20 20	21 29	19 50	19 45	19 40	19 34
60	19 21	20 08	21 10	19 49	19 47	19 46	19 46
N 58	19 15	19 59	20 55	19 47	19 49	19 52	19 56
56	19 10	19 50	20 42	19 46	19 51	19 57	20 05
54	19 05	19 43	20 31	19 44	19 53	20 02	20 13
52	19 01	19 37	20 22	19 43	19 54	20 06	20 20
50	18 57	19 31	20 13	19 42	19 56	20 10	20 26
45	18 48	19 19	19 56	19 40	19 58	20 18	20 40
N 40	18 41	19 09	19 43	19 38	20 01	20 25	20 52
35	18 35	19 01	19 32	19 36	20 03	20 31	21 02
30	18 29	18 54	19 23	19 35	20 05	20 36	21 10
20	18 20	18 43	19 09	19 32	20 08	20 45	21 25
N 10	18 12	18 34	18 59	19 30	20 11	20 53	21 39
0	18 05	18 26	18 50	19 28	20 14	21 01	21 51
S 10	17 58	18 19	18 44	19 25	20 16	21 09	22 04
20	17 50	18 13	18 38	19 23	20 19	21 17	22 17
30	17 42	18 06	18 34	19 20	20 23	21 26	22 33
35	17 37	18 02	18 32	19 19	20 24	21 32	22 42
40	17 31	17 59	18 30	19 17	20 27	21 38	22 52
45	17 25	17 55	18 29	19 15	20 29	21 45	23 04
S 50	17 17	17 50	18 28	19 12	20 32	21 54	23 19
52	17 14	17 48	18 28	19 11	20 33	21 58	23 26
54	17 10	17 46	18 27	19 09	20 35	22 03	23 34
56	17 06	17 44	18 27	19 08	20 37	22 08	23 43
58	17 01	17 41	18 27	19 06	20 38	22 13	23 53
S 60	16 56	17 39	18 27	19 04	20 41	22 20	24 04

Day	SUN Eqn. of Time 00h	12h	Mer. Pass.	MOON Mer. Pass. Upper	Lower	Age	Phase
	m s	m s	h m	h m	h m	d	
25	02 08	01 59	12 02	13 17	00 54	02	
26	01 51	01 43	12 02	14 03	01 40	03	
27	01 34	01 26	12 01	14 50	02 26	04